Critical Democracy and LGBTQ-Inclusive Curriculum

This book illustrates the relationship between politics and the ways in which lesbian, gay, bisexual, transgender, and queer (LGBTQ) issues are taught in schools. This book examines relationships between society, schools, and LGBTQ inclusion in order to understand perennial issues related to critical democratic education, and how schools are responding to generational shifts in ideology. By conducting a case study comparison of California and Utah, Camicia provides an in-depth view of the politically and culturally different landscapes that shape LGBTQ curriculum in schools.

This book will synthesize and extend theoretical frameworks to describe, analyze, and interpret the shifting landscapes in public education as they relate to LGBTQ issues in schools. Through queer theory and democratic education theory, Camicia offers recommendations to public schools and teacher educators about socially just ways to create inclusive LGBTQ curriculum.

Steven P. Camicia is Associate Professor of Teacher Education and Leadership at Utah State University, USA.

Critical Democratic Education and LGBTQ-Inclusive Curriculum

Opportunities and Constraints

Steven P. Camicia

Routledge
Taylor & Francis Group

LONDON AND NEW YORK

First published 2016 by Routledge

2 Park Square, Milton Park, Abingdon, Oxfordshire OX14 4RN

52 Vanderbilt Avenue, New York, NY 10017

Routledge is an imprint of the Taylor & Francis Group, an informa business

First issued in paperback 2020

Copyright © 2016 Taylor & Francis

Library of Congress Cataloguing in Publication Data
A catalog record for this book has been requested

ISBN: 978-0-415-70992-7 (hbk)
ISBN: 978-0-367-54098-2 (pbk)

Typeset in Times New Roman
by Apex CoVantage, LLC

Contents

Preface

Public schools are charged with teaching students how to effectively participate in democratic, multicultural, local, and global communities. This means different things in different communities because schools are embedded in complex networks of power relations. This book examines how different cultural and political landscapes provide opportunities and constraints related to lesbian, gay, bisexual, transgender, and queer (LGBTQ) inclusion and critical democratic education. The purpose of the book is to provide educators and policy makers with a framework for understanding how to increase inclusion and, as a result, increase social justice and critical democratic education in public schools.

Chapter 2 synthesizes lenses of critical democratic theory and education with those of queer theory as a way to view the illustrations presented in the rest of the book. The inclusiveness of democratic education is increased through the lens of queer theory because queer theory is particularly sensitive to the way that LGBTQ issues and individuals are excluded through normalizing discourses of society. Norms are examined as cultural products rather than products of 'nature'. Many of the causes of misrecognition and stereotypes are related to a dominant culture's categorizations of a marginalized culture. These categories and the qualities assigned to them serve to demean and devalue marginalized individuals and their knowledge. Part of the insidiousness of this misrecognition is the ability of a dominant culture to portray such inaccurate portrayals as 'natural'.

Queer theory helps identify the normalizing forces in society that define what is 'natural' and what is 'unnatural'. The various sexual and gendered experiences are not forced into binary oppositions, such as female/male or heterosexual/homosexual, binaries that function to support marginalizing norms. These binaries stand in the way of recognition because those who do not identify or are not identified with the binary construction are viewed as less than human. This is evident in a long history of the portrayal of those who don't 'fit' into these categories as emotionally, mentally, and physically 'sick'. By examining the experiences of LGBTQ individuals in curriculum, students can see that the pathology is in society and not individuals. This pathology takes the form of inequitable social structures of racism, sexism, ableism, heterosexism, classism, nationalism, ethnocentrism, and homophobia. Such ideologies and discourses serve to dehumanize those who are marginalized in such hierarchies. They literally misrecognize those with the least power in order to construct and maintain the privilege of the dominant culture. Critical democratic education is strengthened when students examine the experiences of those who are marginalized and the structures and institutions that are responsible for their marginalization. This increases the number of perspectives in the curriculum and the possible solutions to social inequalities.

Chapters 3 and 4 examine the contexts of Utah and California. My search for examples of democratic and LGBTQ-inclusive curriculum was foreshadowed by an educational policy in the state of California that requires, among other inclusive practices, that LGBT history be taught in public schools (California Legislature, 2011–2012). Known as the FAIR (Fair, Accurate, Inclusive, and Respectful) Act, the policy was in contrast to other policies where the only way students might learn about LGBTQ issues was through antibullying or public health curricula. In contrast to the California example, I sought examples in Utah because of the restrictions and ambiguity involved with state laws surrounding LGBTQ inclusivity in curriculum. An examination of these two educational policy contexts provided an illustration of how school curriculum in general and democratic inclusive curriculum in particular might look different within these two contexts. What might be the consequences for LGBTQ and non-LGBTQ students in these different environments? What might such differences between contexts imply about conceptions of equity and social justice?

Although there have been glimmers of more inclusive policies in Utah, such as the 1990s successful challenge that supported Gay-Straight Alliances,[1] which made national news, educational policy in Utah is particularly restrictive and exclusionary. One policy states, "The following may not be taught in Utah public schools through the use of instructional materials, direct instruction, or online instruction . . . (2) the advocacy of homosexuality . . ." (Utah Division of Administrative Rules, 2014). The wording leaves a level of ambiguity that has a chilling effect upon educators who want to create critical democratic and LGBTQ-inclusive learning environments because educators are left wondering what constitutes "advocacy." Does it apply to teaching about LGBTQ individuals or civil rights movements in history classes? Can language arts courses assign books with LGBTQ characters? When learning about families in younger grades, to what degree are LGBTQ children and parents represented? These are questions that take on an intensified dimension within the context of the socially conservative politics and culture of Utah.

In Utah, I wanted to see how teachers were creating inclusive environments where democratic classroom communities could flourish within this restrictive environment. Instead, I found a culture of fear where if the curriculum in school was LGBTQ inclusive, it was not very visible. I asked university professors in the area of teacher education who prepare students for social studies classrooms and language arts classrooms. I did not receive any nominations or leads for people to participate in my study.

I also asked community organizations that provide LGBTQ-inclusive education outside of schools. As a result of these inquiries, I was able to find three teachers who would interview, but even in progressive communities in Utah, I found no support from school districts. It was at this time that I became aware of a Utah law that restricts teaching, discussion, or research in public schools related to "sexual behavior, orientation, or attitudes" (1c) unless written permission is given by parents (Utah Code: 53A-13–302). This restriction in effect bans students, educators, and researchers from discussing sexual identities because many parents will not give consent for their children to participate in related activities. It was not surprising that although LGBTQ-inclusive afterschool groups were able to meet, there was still little evidence of LGBTQ-inclusive curriculum in classrooms. I received some information that the best place for me to look would be in private schools. Whereas I am relieved that private schools have what people told me is LGBTQ-inclusive curriculum, this inclusion in private schools made the exclusion in public schools all the more disturbing. How could it be that schools that are not public might be more inclusive than schools that have the specific charge of serving the public? As a result of the difficulties in locating inclusivity in Utah schools, I reframed my examination to focus upon the different cultural and political contexts in both states where public school curriculum decisions are made.

In Chapter 5, I compare and contrast the contexts of California and Utah. The comparison between the two is not as simple as a utopian (California) versus dystopian (Utah) view of LGBTQ inclusiveness in curriculum. However, there is a clear difference between the two contexts. These differences have implications related to the legitimacy of public schooling in a democracy. Based upon my illustrations in Chapters 3 and 4, I synthesize a curriculum proposal based upon the inclusionary practices of educators and a framework of inclusion developed by Young (2000). This proposal revolves around the following areas of inclusivity and recognition: transformative rather than additive approaches, third spaces, critical thinking, intersectionality, positionality, power/knowledge, discourse analysis, greeting, rhetoric, and narrative. These areas overlap in a model of transformative curriculum that supports critical democratic and LGBTQ-inclusive education.

In Chapter 6, I conclude the book with a epilogue discussing a rationale for using autoethnography within curriculum in order to increase inclusion. Autoethnography provides an avenue for increasing recognition of students and educators because it uses personal experiences and identities as points of departure for understanding social inequalities within different communities. This results in narratives and counternarratives that increase the number and recognition of individuals and perspectives, which is a key component of critical democratic and LGBTQ-inclusive curriculum. Rather than view discussion as embedded in a decontextualized vacuum, discussion is embedded in power relations that must be examined if social justice is to be addressed in curriculum. I provide my autoethnography as an illustration.

Because local and national laws outside of school policies are becoming more inclusive, schools have an obligation to be responsive to these changes. How is it that communities are able to justify the exclusion of gender identities and sexual identities from the curriculum? What grounds, for example, do schools have to exclude curriculum containing same-sex relationships when national and state laws recognize marriage equality? When schools are out of step with progressive changes in laws and policies within society, the legitimacy of schools serving the interests of students and a public diminishes. With these considerations, I hope to open complicated conversations about increasing LGBTQ-inclusive curriculum that is responsive to the needs of students, educators, guardians, and community members. Rather than avoid the complexities of curriculum and conversation, I propose that communities and the schools that serve them embrace such conversations as matters of educational equity and social justice.

Note

1 In Utah, LGBTQ-inclusive afterschool clubs are named Queer-Straight Alliances.

References

California Legislature: An Act to Amend Sections 51204.5, 51500, 51501, 60040, and 60044 of the Education Code, Relating to Instruction. (2011–2012).

Utah Administrative Code R277–474: School Instruction and Human Sexuality, R277–474–3 C.F.R. § A. (2) (2014).

Young, I. M. (2000). *Inclusion and democracy*. New York: Oxford University Press.

Acknowledgments

This book would not have been possible without many individuals who were generous in providing their time, expertise, and support. I am grateful to the educators who shared their views relating to this project. These include Thomas Adams, Kristen Cruz Allen, Hilary Burge, Tarah Fleming, Kenneth McDonald, Rick Oculto, Don Romesburg, and those participants who preferred to remain anonymous. Their commitments to social justice in education inspired my work. I also want to thank GSA Network, Welcoming Schools, and the California Department of Education. The reviewers Routledge commissioned helped guide some key elements of this book. I appreciate the guidance and patience of Lauren Verity, Christina Chronister, Katherine Tsamparlis, and Karen Adler, my editor. My colleagues in social studies educational research provided support from my professional community: Patricia Avery, Terence Beck, Spencer Clark, Diana Hess, J.B. Mayo, and Walter Parker. Utah State University has been very supportive of my work, particularly my former department head, Martha Dever. I thank my parents, Levi and Diane Allen, who demonstrated unconditional love and encouragement when others around me were not always gracious. Finally, I want to thank my husband, Darrin Brooks, who has loved and nurtured me.

1 Democracy, Inclusion, and Curriculum

The curriculum is a site where the recurring question of the subject[1] is posed, informed by centuries of critical thought and creative scholarship reconstructed through solitary study and complicated conversation.

William F. Pinar (2011, p. 144)

Many societies around the globe are increasing their recognition[2] of LGBTQ[3] individuals. This recognition has been illustrated by the legal recognition of same-sex marriage, which I will refer to as marriage equality from here on. Whereas this is a significant shift in understandings of gender and sexuality, it leaves many LGBTQ individuals and relationships unrecognized by the law. Because marriage in the United States has a history of patriarchy and opposite-sex recognition, relationships that don't mirror this history are framed in terms of patriarchal, heterosexual, and gender conformity. This excludes a vast universe of possibilities related to relationships, gender identities, and sexualities. Although marriage equality is recognized by the United States as part of the 2015 U.S. Supreme Court decision *Obergefell v. Hodges*, there is a long list of discriminatory practices still aimed at LGBTQ individuals. This discrimination is evident in areas such as housing, adoption, employment, heath care, and schooling.

Whereas there is a long way to go toward equality, it is safe to say that there is a trend toward more recognition of LGBTQ individuals and their rights in the United States. With this trend toward more recognition, polls also indicate regional and age differences. These and other differences create a patchwork of various contexts in which students and educators participate in schools. The main questions of this book are: How do public policies around schools respond to shifts toward recognition? What does school resistance to these shifts tell us about the legitimacy of public education? How can we facilitate schools and curriculum that are inclusive and socially just? The connection between recognition and democracy is central to public schools that educate students to participate effectively in local and global multicultural democratic communities. I am using the term recognition similar to the way that we might recognize an acquaintance passing on a street.

One of the main hindrances to democracy is a lack of recognition of individuals in our communities. As I discuss later, whereas the perspectives of marginalized individuals and groups might be added to the conversation, dominant groups often define the rules of inclusion. Structures of communication enact values and modes that reflect dominant cultures or identities in conversation. Because these structures determine the process and content involved in communication, there is little chance that those who are marginalized by these structures can join conversations. Whereas on the surface, communication in public meetings such as school council meetings seems to be structured for equality, forces of power and privilege often determine the limits of who and what gets recognized as legitimate in conversation and deliberations.

Under such conditions, even if a perspective is added to the conversation, the addition is somewhat superficial because it is embedded in a larger structure of communication that reflects dominant assumptions. Curriculum, as a complicated conversation, reflects this phenomenon. Additive approaches to meetings or curriculum do not sufficiently account for the underlying workings of inequitable power relations embedded in communication. One of the ways to address inequitable recognition is to examine the ways that power shapes conversations, deliberations, discourses, curriculum, and forms of recognition. Additive approaches do not address the underlying structures in communication that marginalize the additions of individuals, perspectives, issues, and LGBTQ-inclusive curriculum.

Although some of the illustrations in this book indicate there are places of increasing LGBTQ recognition in curriculum, many other illustrations within this book indicate that schools still lag far behind societal shifts. One of the hazards of writing a book related to societal shifts is that by the time a book goes to print, the statistics become dated,[4] and the book loses some of its relevance. Even worse, those opposed to LGBTQ-inclusive school policies can focus upon lack of current statistics to undermine attempts to make schools more inclusive. Rather than focus upon statistics and quantitative descriptions, the purpose of this book is to examine relationships between society, schools, and LGBTQ inclusion in order to understand perennial issues related to critical democratic education. I interviewed educators and gathered information such as instructional materials, media accounts, and policy documents in two contexts, Utah and California. My purpose for choosing these different contexts was to provide illustrations of the ways that context might influence the degree and type of LGBTQ recognition within public schools and, as a result, critical democratic education. Because the legitimacy of democratic communities is based upon the representation of those who are subject to policies, community members must have a part in the decision-making process. Recognition has a direct bearing upon the legitimacy of our public schools. When students, educators, guardians, and community members are excluded from the curriculum, the legitimacy of public schools is called into question.

Schools can play an important role in making our communities more democratic, but this has to be one of the learning objectives. Students, parents, and educators do not experience schools within a decontextualized social vacuum. Curriculum as expressed through policies, course objectives, instructional materials, pedagogies, and learning activities is designed, implemented, and experienced within the unique contexts of different communities. Because there are differences within and between communities, curriculum looks different from one community to another. In other words, individuals and groups experience the public school curriculum within a variety of historical and contemporary contexts that are influenced by culture and politics. How might these different contexts influence the degree of LGBTQ recognition and critical democratic education in schools?

The dominant political and cultural contexts of Utah and California are different in key areas. Whereas conservatives dominate Utah's politics, progressives dominate California's politics. The political influence of Utah's dominant religion, The Church of Jesus Christ and Latter-day Saints (LDS), intensifies differences around public policy, schools, and LGBTQ issues. California has been at the forefront of social movements and policies aimed at increasing LGBTQ inclusion. Public schools are embedded in these contexts. Policies and curriculum are the result of conversations, deliberations, and discourses occurring within different cultural and political landscapes. These differences have a profound impact upon the ways that students and educators experience public schools.

Utah and California also have a relationship around the issue of marriage equality. The relationship between the two states during California Proposition 8 (2008), which defined marriage as between a man and a woman, illustrated another layer of complexity. Proposition 8 was supported through large contributions from Utah. In effect, the LDS church in Utah influenced the political and legal landscape of California in relation to an LGBTQ issue. Through a well-funded media campaign, the dominant discourses within Utah were played out in California politics. In addition, California's Proposition 8 illustrated regional differences between the largely coastal regions of California that were against the proposition and regions in the middle and eastern part of the state that supported the proposition. This divide illustrates how different communities and their recognition of LGBTQ individuals are more complex than a Utah-bad/California-good comparison. Although dominant discourses within a state influence communication, localized discourses within communities and schools also influence the degree of LGBTQ inclusion. The characteristics of an individual school have a large influence upon the support and inclusion that queer youth experience (Martin-Storey, Cheadle, Skalamera, & Crosnoe, 2015).

Because curriculum mirrors different communities and the power relations within society, issues that cause disagreement in society are often the same issues that cause disagreements over curriculum and public schools. Disagreements occur in all subject areas (Zimmerman, 2002). There are disagreements over how to teach subjects ranging from mathematics to history. Because the power to control curriculum means the power to influence the future of society through what students learn, the intensity of curriculum battles can run passionately and deeply. Different cultural and political landscapes communicate different beliefs about the future of society and what students will learn about the past, present, and future. Apple writes, "The basic framework of most curriculum rationality is generally supportive and accepting of the *existing* economic, political, ideological, and intellectual framework that apportions opportunity and power in American society" (emphaisis in the original, 2004, p. 101). Curriculum reflects the knowledge of what those in positions of power in society deem important, as well as how those in power can maintain their power (Camicia & Franklin, 2016). Curriculum is often a tool that structures values and modes of communication that benefit dominant groups in society at the expense of marginalized groups. Even when marginalized groups and perspectives are added to the curriculum, the additions are embedded within larger discursive forces within the curriculum. These structures within the curriculum benefit dominant groups.

A good place to start examining such structures is to ask who benefits from the content and modes of communication within the curriculum. Which individuals, groups, and organizations, for example, benefit from curriculum decisions that are based upon standardized testing? Who has the most to gain from privileging the knowledge that is tested? Who benefits from standardizing this knowledge across local and global contexts? The answers to these questions are usually associated with the positions of the people who are empowered to make curriculum decisions. If, for example, standardization of curriculum is implemented by those who favor competition in markets over other educational outcomes, those people who benefit most by markets will benefit most from the curriculum (Anyon, 2006). This often comes at the expense of people who place other educational values such as social justice at the forefront of learning objectives.

As another example, history curriculum reflects historical narratives that mirror those of the dominant culture. Curriculum works toward constructing and maintaining a dominant culture's perspectives and perpetuating racism through history curriculum (Leonardo & Grubb, 2014). The curriculum represents a particular worldview that communicates society's past, present, and hopes for the future (Pinar, 2004). It is no wonder that differing beliefs about the past, present, and future of society cause disagreements over curriculum. As it relates to LGBTQ recognition, who benefits from excluding LGBTQ individuals and perspectives from the history curriculum? Who benefits from curriculum tailored toward prohibiting conversations and discourses surrounding sexualities and gender identities as they have historically been expressed throughout history? When these questions are not asked, the curriculum serves the interest of those who identify and are identified with dominant forms of sexuality and gender identity.

Inclusion and exclusion in curriculum structure the conversations and discourse within schools. Given that public schools have finite resources and time, the curriculum cannot contain the entire universe of knowledge. Decisions must be made on what is included and excluded from the curriculum. What is included in the curriculum sends a powerful message to students, but what is excluded can send just as powerful a message (Eisner, 2002). In a subject such as history, decisions need to be made about which historical figures are or are not represented in the curriculum. When individuals and groups are included, how are they represented or misrepresented? What do these inclusions, exclusions, representations, and misrepresentations communicate about what individuals and groups are valued by society over others? The answers to these questions are grounded in historical and contemporary power relations between individuals and groups and their relative abilities to control the curriculum. On the level of communication, the answers to these questions indicate what can and can't be said about social injustices of transphobia, sexism, and homophobia. Although significant forces shape past and present lives and society, these exclusionary networks of power relations and the dominant groups they benefit go unexamined in curriculum.

In order for schools to increase LGBTQ inclusion and recognition in the curriculum, they need to move past the simple addition of perspectives to the curriculum toward a more transformative approach (Banks, 1994; Camicia, 2007). Transformation involves an examination of the dominant narratives that structure the ways that students understand the world. Rather than representing social studies subjects such as geography, civics, economics, and history as centering on a few individuals, the influences of institutions, social groups, and the discourses that validate these subject areas need to be examined. Illustrations throughout this book provide snapshots of the ways that curriculum can move toward a transformative curriculum that aims to increase social justice by questioning the dominant discourses that structure what can and can't be known in schools.

When I started research for this book, I planned to work inside and outside of schools to find examples of critical democratic education that were LGBTQ inclusive. My reasoning was that positive examples could be helpful for those who would like to design and implement such a curriculum. I chose the different political contexts of Utah and California in order to highlight the different ways that critical democratic and LGBTQ-inclusive education is reflected in educational policy and curriculum. Different contexts provide a larger range of perspectives concerning how educators and policy makers move toward transformative curriculum within different opportunities and constraints.

Although the aim of my search was to look for examples of critical democratic education and inclusion, examples of exclusionary and undemocratic education were one of the by-products of my search. I was not completely surprised by these exclusionary practices, but I was somewhat surprised by the variety of methods used by those seeking to exclude LGBTQ individuals from the curriculum. Whereas I found some teachers who incorporate inclusivity in their curriculum, the surrounding policies or communities in which their teaching was embedded restricted the visibility of their work. Rather than focus upon individual classrooms, I decided to focus upon the histories, contexts, and policies that help or hinder inclusivity. The result was an illustration of how inclusion and exclusion form dynamic webs of power relations that influence students and teachers inequitably within and across communities. It is within these webs of power relations that curriculum and the discourses that influence them are planned and implemented.

My examination is not meant to be representative of large populations, but it provides snapshots of inclusion, recognition, equity, exclusion, and inequity that can inform conversations aimed toward improving educational equity and the lives of LGBTQ students and educators. My hope is that the illustrations I provide from Utah and California will open conversations about critical democratic and LGBTQ-inclusive education that might transfer[5] to other situations and contexts. In order to increase the degree of transferability to a variety of contexts, I interpret the themes of transformative curriculum that can guide planning and implementation across the social studies content areas.

Rather than conversations about how to add identity groups to the curriculum, I hope to open conversations that transform the overarching narrative of the curriculum toward social justice. This is why I use the term 'critical' to modify the term 'democratic'. An examination of inequitable power relations as is implied by the word critical is necessary in democratic education that fosters social justice. I also hope that these conversations will occur among a wide variety of stakeholders such as preservice teachers, teacher educators, in-service teachers, K-12 students, parents, administrators, community leaders, and educational policy makers. These curriculum conversations are likely to be, in Pinar's words, "complicated" (2011, p. 144). However, if we avoid the complexity of these conversations, we are in effect maintaining an inequitable status quo. The only people who stand to gain from such avoidance are dominant groups whose objective is to bolster a curriculum that reflects their worldviews and interests.

Because curriculum is embedded in the unique historical and contemporary milieus of knowledge, societies, individuals, and groups, conversations about curriculum are bound to be complicated. Issues of critical democracy and LGBTQ inclusivity are some of the most complicated, and when applied to public education settings, contentiousness intensifies. When applied to public education settings, this contentiousness intensifies. Schools can become a stage for different stakeholders to air their differences. Although schools are accountable to multiple stakeholders, students are affected most by decisions. This often makes schools dangerous for LGBTQ students because those wishing to exclude them from the curriculum are harming them emotionally, mentally, and physically (Kosciw, Greytak, Palmer, & Boesen, 2014). Laws, policies, and regulations that are LGBTQ inclusive or exclusive have an influence upon school climate (Kull, Kosciw, & Greytak, 2015). Students in schools that are not guided by LGBTQ-inclusive laws, policies, and regulations are more likely to experience a negative and unsafe school climate (Burdge, Sinclair, Laub, & Russell, 2012). The exclusion of someone with a marginalized identity is disproportionate to those who are not excluded because those who are included in curriculum and policies are identified with a dominant identity. Rather than decontextualizing reasons in the public debate, discussions over inclusion or exclusion are personal. They are very personal. Being excluded from the curriculum has personal consequences for LGBTQ students, teachers, administrators, families, and community members.

Historical and contemporary discrimination against LGBTQ individuals is a complicated and ever-changing reflection of inequitable power relations. Those with power are privileged through laws and norms. This privilege has been afforded to heterosexual individuals and individuals who identify with the gender they were assigned at birth. Individuals with sexual orientations or gender identities that do not align with heterosexual or cisgender[6] identities face discrimination and exclusion. When issues of inclusion and exclusion of LGBTQ individuals in society enter into curriculum conversations, the conversations are complicated. When they do not enter into these public conversations, such conversations operate to silence LGBTQ individuals, making the curriculum an even more oppressive and complicated conversation. The message is clear in such conversations: heterosexual and cisgender individuals are reflected in the curriculum as a norm that functions to devalue the lives and experiences of LGBTQ individuals and issues. These exclusionary practices mark a community as undemocratic because the will of the powerful is used to silence the less powerful. Because some of those who are subject to curriculum do not have a voice in the curriculum, it is undemocratic. An exclusionary curriculum communicates the quality and will of an undemocratic community to all students.

In contrast to exclusionary practices, one of the defining qualities of a democratic community is the ability for *every* person in the community to be included in public conversations that influence their lives. The legitimacy of democratic governance is directly tied to the ability of all who are affected by a decision to be included in the decision-making process. Harding (1993) writes, "An effective pursuit of democracy requires that those who bear the consequences of decisions have a proportionate share in making them" (p. 3). Ideally, public schools are places where students can experience how to participate in democratic communities in this inclusive way. Students enter classrooms and interact with people who have different identities, experiences, and perspectives. These differences provide a space where students can learn how to create inclusive and democratic communities. Through communicating these differences, students and teachers have the opportunity to expand their appreciation of a public sphere where differences are recognized, discussed, and valued.

The focus of this book is on critical democratic education and the ways that LGBTQ individuals are recognized and included or excluded from the curriculum. LGBTQ students benefit from this inclusion by seeing themselves in curriculum and knowing that when they speak, their LGBTQ identities are recognized along with their other identities. Carlson (1998) writes, "To refuse to see or recognize the identity of those who have been oppressed or discriminated against because of that identity is to deny that oppression and discrimination exist" (p. 95). The recognition of students with marginalized identities such as LGBTQ students is an important component of socially conscious and equity-oriented critical democratic education.

In addition to the benefits to LGBTQ students, non-LGBTQ students are able to recognize differences within their midst by learning about various perspectives. This is especially true when discussing social issues. Although social issues are often the text of social studies education, these issues can be discussed in multiple subject areas. As diversity is recognized, the possible solutions to social issues are expanded. Students embodying dominant identities are afforded the opportunity to see the value in having more information and choices in a democracy. The multiple perspectives that emerge support a generation of curriculum standards such as the College, Career, and Civic Life (C3) and Common Core State Standards (CCSS). These standards recommend that students grapple with multiple perspectives as a way to increase the depth of their understanding and critical thinking skills.

Critical democratic education and principles of inclusion are important qualities of democratic school governance (e.g., educational policy and administration). Democratic school governance recognizes the voices of students, guardians, parents, and educators concerning what students learn and how they learn it. One of the objectives of this approach is to produce, facilitate, and maintain a learning environment designed for *all* students to learn how to participate effectively in democratic communities. A critical democratic education recognizes differences that are silenced or misrepresented by dominant society. Differences of race, ethnicity, class, ability, language, geopolitical belonging, gender, and sexual orientation intersect in dynamic and complex ways on the bodies of students and educators. This intersection creates a position where each person experiences and understands the world in unique ways, a phenomenon that is referred to as positionality. For example, a same-sex couple might view marriage uniquely based upon past experiences of discrimination. These experiences of discrimination could lead to a unique understanding of what marriage means and how their right to marry or not means something different to them than people in an opposite-sex relationship. Positionality is relational. Same-sex relationships and opposite-sex relationships are situated within the societal context of power relations. This is evident in the way that society has historically offered more legal and monetary benefits to opposite-sex marriages. The position of an opposite-sex married couple is related to society differently than the position of a same-sex married couple. Expressing this relational view of positionality, Maher and Tetreault (1993) write:

> Gender, race, class, and other aspects of our identities are markers of relational positions rather than essential qualities. Knowledge is valid when it includes an acknowledgment of the knower's specific position in any context, because changing contextual and relational factors are crucial for defining identities and our knowledge in any given situation.
>
> (p. 118)

The recognition of positionality is an important component of critical democratic education because the expressions of students and teachers are contextualized as historical and relational. In addition, the subjects of geography, history, economics, and civics can be viewed through these relational lenses. Rather than, for example, interpreting a historical narrative as decontextualized, the narrative can gain depth by using the lenses of race, ethnicity, gender identity, sexual identity, language, ability, and geopolitical belonging. This focus upon meaning and knowledge as relational is an important part of an education for critical democracy because students recognize difference on a deeper level in order to better understand both differences and commonalities. Without this recognition, knowledge is perceived as neutral rather than the product of cultural and political interests. When this recognition is absent, commonalities are defined by the dominant culture and differences are subsumed under a false pretense of 'neutrality'.

An authentic critical democratic education requires that students and educators take into account how the strength of a person's voice in a democratic community reflects the relative power of the person who is speaking. This is due to the norms of dominant identities that recognize some people as of less value than others. One of the most illustrative examples of this in curriculum is the absence of historical accounts of marginalized individuals and groups in textbooks. Even when marginalized individuals and groups are included, the inclusion is superficial and it does not challenge dominant cultural and political narratives. If a relational aspect of recognition is not examined in schools, dominant voices drown out marginalized voices. This is why inclusive and critical democratic education relies upon an examination of positionality and related power inequities within educational communities, as well as communities outside of school. This type of curriculum emphasizes transformation rather than addition. In other words, rather than add narratives of marginalized individuals, the curriculum transforms the dominant narrative through an examination of power relations. The resulting curriculum is critically democratic and inclusive.

Notes

1 Pinar (2011) makes it clear that "subjects" are to be considered as including both the academic areas and the individuals who experience the curriculum. He writes, "The subject—in both its meanings as person and as school subject—has been central to rather different conceptions of education" (p. xii). In the concluding lines of his book, he writes, "Mythological and singular, past and present, private and public, the subject (in both its senses) is allegorical. From such temporally structured and historically informed 'double consciousness' we can reconstruct the character of curriculum studies" (p. 144). I explore this concept more in my concluding chapter.

2 The term "recognition" can be used in multiple ways (i.e., legal recognition, recognition to speak in a meeting, and recognizing a face). These forms of recognition are often intertwined and form one of the main ideas of the book. Recognition is a concept, perception, and action that will developed throughout this book.

3 I follow the lead of Mayo (2014) who uses "LGBTQ to include a wide range of gender and sexual minorities" (p. 1, n. 1). Mayo further clarifies that some authors quoted in the text use other terms. When quoting authors throughout this book, I will retain their terms.

4 For current quantitative research about LGBTQ students, see reports by the Gay, Lesbian and Straight Education Network (GLSEN), http://glsen.org/nscs.

5 In qualitative research, sample size is usually small, and the objective is to generalize to similar cases rather than generalize to a larger population. For a discussion of this distinction, see Yin (2003). This type of generalizability is also referred to as transference because findings from one qualitative study can inform other cases with similar phenomenon and contexts. Also see (Cresswell, 2013, pp. 244–253; Guba & Lincoln, 2005, pp. 205–209).

6 Cisgender describes people who identify with the gender that they were assigned at birth.

References

Anyon, J. (2006). Social class, school knowledge, and the hidden curriculum: Retheorizing reproduction. In L. Weis, C. McCarthy & G. Dimitriadis (Eds.), *Ideology, curriculum, and the new sociology of education* (pp. 37–45). New York: Routledge.

Apple, M. W. (2004). *Ideology and curriculum* (3rd ed.). New York: Routledge Falmer.

Banks, J. A. (1994). Transforming the mainstream curriculum. *Educational Leadership, 51*(8), 4–8.

Burdge, H., Sinclair, K., Laub, C., & Russell, S. T. (2012). *Lessons that matter: LGBTQ inclusivity and school safety*. San Francisco, CA: Gay-Straight Alliance Network and California Safe Schools Coaltion Report No. 14.

Camicia, S. P. (2007). Deliberating immigration policy: Locating instructional materials within global and multicultural perspectives. *Theory and Research in Social Education, 35*(1), 96–111.

Camicia, S. P., & Franklin, B. M. (2016). Michael W. Apple, ideology and curriculum (1979). In J. L. DeVitis (Ed.), *Popular educational classics: A reader* (pp. 109–119). New York: Peter Lang.

Carlson, D. (1998). Who am I? Gay identitiy and a democratic politics of the self. In W. F. Pinar (Ed.), *Queer theory in education* (pp. 92–101). Mahwah, NJ: Lawrence Erlbaum Associates, Publishers.

Cresswell, J. W. (2013). *Qualitative inquiry and research design: Choosing among five approaches* (3rd ed.). London: Sage.

Eisner, E. W. (2002). *The educational imagination: On the design and evaluation of school programs* (3rd ed.). Upper Saddle River, NJ: Prentice Hall.

Guba, E. G., & Lincoln, Y. S. (2005). Paradigmatic controversies, contradictions, and emerging confluences. In N. K. Denzin & Y. S. Lincoln (Eds.), *The SAGE handbook of qualitative research* (3rd ed., pp. 191–215). Thousand Oaks, CA: Sage Publications.

Harding, S. (Ed.). (1993). *The "racial" economy of science: Toward a democratic future*. Bloomington, IN: Indiana University Press.

Kosciw, J. G., Greytak, E. A., Palmer, N. A., & Boesen, M. J. (2014). *The 2013 national school climate survey: The experiences of lesbian, gay, bisexual and transgender youth in our nation's schools*. New York: GLSEN (Gay, Lesbian & Straight Education Network).

Kull, R. M., Kosciw, J. G., & Greytak, E. A. (2015). *From statehouse to schoolhouse: Anti-bullying policy efforts in the U.S. states and school districts*. New York: GLSEN (Gay, Lesbian & Straight Education Network).

Leonardo, Z., & Grubb, N. W. (2014). *Education and racism: A primer on issues and dilemmas*. New York: Routledge.

Maher, F. A., & Tetreault, M. K. (1993). Frames of positionality: Constructing meaningful dialogues about gender and race. *Anthropological Quarterly, 66*(3), 118–126.

Martin-Storey, A., Cheadle, J. E., Skalamera, J., & Crosnoe, R. (2015). Exploring the social integration of sexual minority youth across high school contexts. *Child Development, 86*(3), 965–975.

Mayo, C. (2014). *LGBTQ youth and education: Policies and practices*. New York: Teachers Collge Press.

Pinar, W. F. (2004). *What is curriculum theory?* Mahwah, NJ: Lawrence Erlbaum Associates, Inc. Publishers.

Pinar, W. F. (2011). *The character of curruiculum studies: Bildung, currere, and the recurring question of the subject*. New York: Palgrave Macmillan.

Yin, R. K. (2003). *Case study research: Design and methods* (3rd ed.). Thousand Oaks, CA: Sage Publications.

Zimmerman, J. (2002). *Whose America?: Culture wars in the public schools*. Cambridge, MA: Harvard University Press.

2   Democratic Education and Queer Theory in Public Schools

"Queer," to me, refers to a politics that values the ways in which meanings and institutions can be at loose ends with each other, crossing all kinds of boundaries rather than reinforcing them. What if the most productive junctures weren't the ones where *everything means the same thing?*

(Sedgwick, 2011, p. 200, emphasis in the original)

Very fragile experiments in democracy could well depend on not just the character and virtue of the citizens but also the ability to be multicontextual in the various frameworks and reason-giving activities in public spaces.

(West, 2011, p. 93)

An underlying assumption of democracy and democratic education is that those influenced by curriculum have a voice in that curriculum (Apple & Beane, 2007; Camicia, 2009). Habermas (1994) writes, "A correctly understood theory of rights requires a politics of recognition that protects the integrity of the individual in the life contexts in which his or her identity is formed" (p. 113). This recognition is necessarily a "complicated conversation" around curriculum (Pinar, 2011, p. 144), but without these conversations, schools are bound to maintain and construct social inequalities. Curriculum is a reflection of a system that regulates what knowledge is deemed valuable and what knowledge is not (Apple, 2004). When voices and perspectives are excluded from curriculum, democratic education suffers. In this chapter, I use concepts in critical democratic and queer theories as rationales for increasing the intelligibility or recognition of perspectives that are often excluded from curriculum. This chapter provides rationales for LGBTQ-inclusive curriculum, as well as a framework for interpreting the cases of California and Utah.

Queer theory emerged from understanding that the experiences and identities of LGBTQ individuals resist categories. Although categories have been politically important for securing LGBTQ rights,[1] categories also function to exclude. LGBTQ experiences and identities intersect and defy definition. These experiences and identities also intersect with identities of race, ethnicity, class, ability, language, and geopolitical belonging. An education that is democratic in both practices and objectives would recognize this variety within the historical and contemporary contexts of social inequalities. The subjects of geography, economics, history, and citizenship education are well aligned with student investigations that recognize students, educators, and communities as they are embedded in these social inequalities. Social studies education is often the place where students experience LGBTQ-inclusive curriculum (Snapp, Burdge, Licona, Moody, & Russell, 2015).

Recognition requires that students and educators uncover unjust and socially constructed hierarchies related to race, ethnicity, class, gender, sexuality, ability, language, and geopolitical belonging. Whereas each of these structures can be examined in isolation, it is the intersection of these oppressive structures that blurs boundaries and intensifies oppression. This is a concept referred to as intersectionality. The bodies of students and educators are embedded in specific locations, histories, lived experiences, and social inequalities that are inscribed uniquely upon them. In other words, each person, historically or contemporarily, is embedded in a unique context that is defined by social relations. This can be described as a person's positionality, which is a complex intersection of perceived and actual identities as they are embedded in socially constructed hierarchies. A transformative and socially just curriculum encourages the blurring of boundaries and favors an examination of power/knowledge as it relates to positionality. This is an important part of critical democratic education because students examine power/knowledge within a wide array of LGBTQ experiences and ways of knowing. As a result, students and educators are recognized for their unique positionalities and perspectives.

This chapter examines the ways that educators might synthesize principles of critical democratic education with principles of queer theory in order to understand the ways that the context of schooling is connected with curriculum. I used the term 'critical' earlier to emphasize that democratic education does not take place within a 'neutral' vacuum of knowledge, reasons, and practices. Instead, power relations permeate the knowledge, reasons, and practices in social settings. This is true historically, geographically, economically, and civically, which makes such awareness central to social studies curriculum that has a social justice orientation. Discussion and decision making in classrooms occur within contexts where dominant voices and categories are valued more than nondominant voices and categories. A queer and democratic space would diminish these exclusions by examining norms, power/knowledge, and exclusion.

Conceptions of queer theory are broad and sometimes contradictory (Haschemi Yekani, Kilian, & Michaelis, 2013). This contentiousness is due to the way that queer theory seeks to destabilize fixed meanings and categories as 'natural' or 'normal'. In order to better understand how these meanings function to exclude individuals, perspectives, and ways of knowing, our understandings of 'natural' or 'normal' categories must be examined. This is also true with the category or identity of queer. When the meanings of queer and queer theory become normalized and fixed, these meanings can be similar to other fixed meanings that exclude (Ferguson, 2013). Hall (2003) writes, "If it is to retain its ability to abrade the 'natural,' queer must be continuously denaturalized itself. And this means posing and continuing to pose some very hard questions about its omissions, blind spots, normal practices, and nervous avoidances" (p. 88).

It is within this critical, self-reflexive space where students and educators struggle with curriculum that perpetuates the norms of institutions and systems through the exclusion of marginalized individuals as outside of the norm and not valued by institutions and systems. This perspective on norms extends to race, class, gender, sexual orientation, ability, language, and geopolitical belonging. Norms perpetuate a dominant identity within each of these as a standard and nondominant identities as outside of the norm and deficient in some way. For example, the category of homosexuality was developed in the nineteenth century by the legal and medical professions to delineate the normal from those outside of the norm (Foucault, 1990, 2003). The legal and medical professions function together in ways that increased the power of norms to define abnormality and ossify social inequalities. In other words, there exist systemic power relations that are dynamic and that operate through institutions such as courts, hospitals, schools, and prisons (Foucault, 1995, 2009). The dramatic changes in how the fields of medicine, psychiatry, and law define what is normal related to gender and sexual identities indicate the way that power/knowledge functions within a dynamic network of power relations (Halperin, 1995).[2] As sites for examination within the various social studies disciplines, these and other institutions and structures provide material for critical thinking oriented toward social justice.

Within power/knowledge systems, norms are defined within institutions and systems such as psychiatry in ways that leave norms unexamined, taken for granted, and natural. This functioning of norms keeps nondominant identities from being recognized because the dominant lens is one of deficit when in actuality deficits rest in institutions, structures, and societies. A focus upon power/knowledge brings attention to the ways that institutions and systems are deficient rather than categorizing individuals as deficient because they do not fit within norms. Halperin (1995) writes, "Queer is by definition *whatever* is at odds with the normal, the legitimate, the dominant. *There is nothing in particular to which it necessarily refers.* It is an identity without an essence" (italics in original, p. 62). A critical democratic social studies curriculum seeks to change the focus from deficient individuals to deficient norms, institutions, systems, and societies that frame individuals as deficient.

Democratic Education: Who Are You?

Democratic education and queer theory overlap in meanings and intentions. These overlaps occur in what can be described as third spaces (Bhabha, 2009). Soja (2009) writes that third spaces are "an invitation to enter a space of extraordinary openness, a place of critical exchange where geographical imagination can be expanded to encompass a multiplicity of perspectives that have heretofore been considered by the epistemological referees to be incompatible, uncombinable" (p. 51). Students and educators are embedded in institutions and systems that reflect power/knowledge relations that perpetuate norms and categorize some as normal and some as deficient. A third space presents possibilities to communicate and imagine possibilities that defy the norms that exclude and marginalize individuals and their perspectives.

As I discussed in Chapter 1, curriculum in schools reflects dominant ideologies and perspectives. Critical democratic education and queer theory highlight the varieties of perspectives that make up our social world, as well as systemic power relations that define what perspectives are of little value. A variety of perspectives is rarely expressed in the curriculum because dominant groups maintain knowledge in the curriculum to reflect their interests. Individuals and groups are embedded in knowledge/power systems that favor some individuals and groups over others. Dominant ideologies perpetuate a taken-for-granted perspective of knowledge in the curriculum. Although there are multiple forms of knowledge, the curriculum reflects the knowledge of those in power. Knowledge is decontextualized and depoliticized in a way that hides the contentious nature of knowledge itself (Apple, 2004). A move toward decontextualization and depoliticalization serves the interest of dominant ideologies, perspectives, discourses, and individuals because knowledge is seen as 'natural' and 'commonsense' rather than a product of society. As Apple points out, this is a view on knowledge that runs counter to what we know about how, for example, scientific communities develop knowledge. They do so in a way that favors contention as a movement toward new knowledge. Social movements shape communities and are almost always contentious because the knowledge that they communicate is deemed unrecognizable to dominant ideologies, discourses, perspectives, individuals, and groups. In this way, the power/knowledge connection in the curriculum functions at the level of epistemology.

A queer and critical democratic curriculum opens a third space where multiple epistemologies are expressed and examined. Epistemologies are central to an understanding of democratic and queer spaces because they refer to different ways of knowing and understanding. Collins (2000) writes that epistemology explains "*why* we believe what we believe to be true. Far from being the apolitical study of truth, epistemology points to the ways in which power relations shape who is believed and why" (p. 252, emphasis in the original). This can be framed within the context of curriculum by asking, *Who is believed in the curriculum and why?* The "epistemological referees" that Soja (2009) refers to earlier can include educators, policy makers, and disciplinary experts who exclude nondominant perspectives and ways of knowing in favor of a dominant or fixed way of knowing.

Queer perspectives help us see how norms exclude, and critical democratic perspectives help us see how exclusion limits perspectives and impedes social justice. Mayo's (2013) study of a Gay-Straight Alliance (GSA) illustrates how third spaces can develop in schools where students have access to knowledge of queer issues, opportunities for activism, reflections on personal experiences, and supportive educators. In this type of school context, the variety of experiences and identities of LGBTQ youth are increased. As a result, the climate of such a school is more democratic. GSAs can often serve as third spaces where LGBTQ youth are recognized (Lapointe, in press; Russell, Muraco, Subramaniam, & Laub, 2009; Russell, Toomey, Crockett, & Laub, 2010). In this book, I look for ways that the context of schooling interacts with the opportunities and constraints within the curriculum and third spaces.

The legitimacy of democracy depends upon the degree to which those who are affected by decisions are included in the decision-making process (Benhabib, 1996; Cohen, 1989; Habermas, 1996; Harding, 1993; Young, 2000). According to Butler (2015), Arent (1958) observed that the question of "Who are you?" is vital to participatory democracy. The recognition of individuals and groups is central to authenticity and social justice in a critical democracy. In social studies subject areas, this recognition creates a more nuanced understanding of historical and contemporary relations. Dialogues in third spaces are avenues for addressing the question of "Who are you?" because through dialogues we are better able to recognize each other when power/knowledge is acknowledged in conversation. For example, student discussions of LGBTQ history and current events can open third spaces in classrooms when the positionalities of students and educators are acknowledged. Are marginalized individuals and groups within the classroom silenced during discussion of these historical and contemporary events related to LGBTQ issues? This space might require, as Boler (2004) describes, an affirmative action pedagogy that privileges marginalized voices related to race, ethnicity, gender identity, sexual identity, class, ability, language, and geopolitical belonging.

The legitimacy of curriculum that teaches students to participate in a democracy is similarly related to the degree in which all affected by a curriculum have a voice in the curriculum (Camicia, 2009, 2014). The following questions illustrate some of the possibilities for students and educators to ask for a better understanding of power/knowledge, norms, and social inequalities: *Who benefits from standardized curriculum and assessments? Whose knowledge is privileged in curriculum? What do the answers to these questions tell us about the relationship of power/knowledge? What might a democratic, queer third space look like in classrooms and curriculum?* These types of questions provide the opportunity for students to open third spaces where dominant norms are examined and perspectives are multiplied.

In order to create a more just curriculum, all students need to be recognized in the curriculum. Unfortunately, multiple forms of exclusion in the curriculum work to limit LGBTQ perspectives and recognition. But educators can shape curriculum and learning environments in ways that increase the inclusion of LGBTQ individuals and groups. This inclusion should consider perspectives of LGBTQ students, guardians, educators, community members, and issues. For example, when these perspectives are recognized in a curriculum that has excluded them, the curriculum becomes more democratic.

Before examining inclusion and recognition in curriculum, it is helpful to understand exclusion and lack of recognition. Young (2000) provides a useful framework for identifying exclusion. She refers to two ways in which people are excluded or not recognized in communication: *external exclusion* and *internal exclusion*. External exclusion is when individuals or groups are denied access to decision-making conversations. This can happen when rules limit participation to a few individuals or dominant groups. Young writes, "*External* exclusion names the many ways that individuals and groups that ought to be included are purposely or inadvertently left out of fora for discussion and decision-making" (p. 52, emphasis in the original). According to Young, most democratic theory is devoted to addressing the problem of external exclusion.

Curriculum reflects external exclusion when marginalized people or perspectives are not allowed in the social studies curriculum. For example, in his analysis of two sets of popular instructional materials on immigration policy, Camicia (2007) found that although the instructional materials claim to represent multiple perspectives, by examining the materials through multicultural and global lenses, he found that they represent a narrow, limited range of perspectives on immigration policy.

Because students are denied these perspectives, it can be said that the instructional materials reflect an external exclusion of cultural and global perspectives. Because racism and immigration policy is rarely addressed and homophobia and immigration policy is never addressed, the perspectives of those marginalized by such policies are excluded from the instructional materials. Because nationalism is not discussed, the instructional materials favor immigration policy that enriches the United States. This functions to exclude reasons for human migration that are larger than those in the interest of the United States. The external exclusion in this example is undemocratic because students are not presented a range of perspectives.

This type of external exclusion related to LGBTQ individuals and issues is prevalent in schools across the United States (Kosciw, Greytak, Palmer, & Boesen, 2014; Kull, Kosciw, & Greytak, 2015). Although students and educators walk into classrooms with multiple perspectives, educators and policy makers have not given their perspectives a public place in the curriculum. External exclusion such as this can be remedied by constructing a curriculum that includes LGBTQ perspectives. For example, educators and students can actively seek a wide variety of perspectives on laws and norms that discriminate against LGBTQ individuals and include them in the curriculum. The new generation of standards, such as the CCSS, emphasizes multiple perspectives in the curriculum. Standards such as these provide another rationale for increasing the recognition of LGBTQ perspectives in curriculum.

Internal exclusion can be more difficult to identify because it functions through norms, discourse, language, and meaning. Young (2000) writes that internal exclusion refers to the way that "the terms of discourse make assumptions some do not share, the interaction privileges specific styles of expression, the participation of some is dismissed as out of order" (p. 53). A speaker who is being internally excluded in this situation is rendered unrecognizable. This is often accomplished by educators and policy makers by appeals to the 'neutrality' of reason, but the neutrality of reason is a myth. Young writes:

> The ideal of disembodied and disembedded reason that it presupposes is a fiction. What such privileging takes to be neutral, universal, and dispassionate expression actually carries the rhetorical nuances of particular situated social positions and relations, which social conventions do not mark as rhetorical and particular in the same way they notice others.
>
> (p. 63)

When individuals or groups do not share the privileged positions and modes of communication that dominant groups express and value, they are rendered unrecognizable. This is evident in the curriculum. For example, curriculum routinely regulates and limits speech surrounding LGBTQ issues involving gender and sexualities (Klein, Markowitz, Puchner, & Anderson, 2011; Kosciw et al., 2014; Sokoll, 2013). The limits of what can and can't be said about gender and sexualities are defined by the dominant culture. Queer identities are externally and internally excluded from subject areas such as history and geography because they are not publicly present, and speech is regulated in such a way that they are not allowed to emerge from curriculum and classroom discussion.

Knowledge is socially constructed and an effect of power. The curriculum reflects this relationship in the ways that it externally and internally excludes LGBTQ perspectives from recognition. Even when marginalized perspectives are included in the curriculum through an attempt to address external exclusion, the curriculum is embedded within a larger context of language and discourse. Referring to Foucault's description of discourse, Stuart Hall (2001) writes that discourse:

> Defines and produces the objects of our knowledge. It governs the way that a topic can be meaningfully talked about and reasoned about. It also influences how ideas are put into practice and used to regulate the conduct of others. Just as a discourse 'rules in' certain ways of talking about a topic, defining an acceptable and intelligible way to talk, write, or conduct oneself, so also, by definition, it 'rules out', limits and restricts other ways of talking, of conducting ourselves in relation to the topic or constructing knowledge about it.
>
> (p. 72)

Because the curriculum reflects institutions, systems, and dominant groups, the discourses of nondominant identities are not allowed into the curriculum. As a result, the curriculum is undemocratic and perpetuates social inequalities. In the study that I discussed earlier (Camicia, 2007), the discourses of monoculturalism and nationalism exclude the discourses of multiculturalism and cosmopolitanism in the instructional materials. In addition to an external exclusion, the instructional materials reflect an internal exclusion because, as Young (2000) writes, "the participation of some is dismissed as out of order" (p. 53). When discussing gender and sexuality in classrooms, cisgender, transphobic, heteronormative, and homophobic discourses regulate what can be spoken and known.

Fortunately, discourses do not act in isolation. Instead, discourses interact upon a discursive field where other discourses also operate (Camicia & Franklin, 2010; Camicia & Zhu, 2011; Snow, 2004; Spillman, 1995; Steinberg, 1999). The relative strengths of each discourse are different. Some discourses have more influence over the rules of what can be spoken, written, and known than other discourses. Weedon (1999) writes:

> In place of Truth, we find a range of competing discourses which make truth claims. For example, the natural and social sciences and religion make claims to the truth of their versions of what gender difference means. The competing discourses which constitute the discursive field are equivalent neither in their explanatory power nor in their effects . . . They are hierarchized by the relations of power which inhere within the discursive fields, privileging some versions and voices over others. Who and what is privileged is an ongoing site of political struggle.
>
> (p. 108)

Because discourses are a reflection of dominant social norms, discourses surrounding race, class, language, gender, sexuality, ability, ethnicity, and geopolitical belonging are regulated by discourses that favor dominant groups. A critical democratic and queer curriculum privileges less powerful or marginalized discourses in order to challenge dominant discourses. Discourses surrounding school social events enforce heteronormative, cisgendered, and patriarchal norms through rules governing writing, speech, knowledge, and actions. One such rule states that sexuality in schools is discussed in clinical terms and relates only to sexually transmitted infections, reproduction, and abstinence (Klein et al., 2011).

By questioning and examining the rules that govern what can and can't be said about gender and sexualities, the curriculum increases recognition of LGBTQ individuals. For example, students can discuss binary constructions of male/female and heterosexual/homosexual. Binary oppositions often favor one side of the binary over the other (Carlson, 1998; Delgado & Stefancic, 2012; Derrida, 1981; Haraway, 1988). Meyer (2012) writes that queer theory "questions taken-for-granted assumptions about relationships, identity, gender, and sexuality. It seeks to explode rigid normalizing categories into possibilities that exist beyond the binaries of black/white, man/woman, disabled/able-bodied, masculine/feminine, student/teacher, gay/straight" (p. 9). Taken-for-granted assumptions in schools and school governance have an enormous impact upon who is valued and recognized. For example, if a male expresses gender in a way that appears feminine, he is literally unrecognizable because the binary constructions of dominant cultures and discourses are challenged.

Intelligibility/Recognition

Recognizing and being recognized are the basis of a critical democratic education. Because *recognition* is a term that runs throughout this book, a description of how I am using it is in order. There are many meanings for the term recognition. Although they are related, the different meanings emphasize different things. One form of recognition is legal recognition. For example, at a certain age, a legal system can recognize a person as an adult. Another form of recognition can involve the receipt of praise. For example, a person can receive an award recognizing excellence in his or her area of expertise. The form of recognition that I thread throughout this book involves intelligibility. For example, one person recognizes someone passing on the street. This form of recognition emphasizes the process by which the qualities that a person possesses are to some degree intelligible to another person. Using queer and critical democratic lenses, these qualities go beyond categories and are constantly in flux, contingent and embedded in power relations (Camicia, 2012; Camicia & Bayon, 2012). Rather than trying to name and categorize, as is usually the case in dominant modes of pedagogy, the process that I describe encourages students and educators to question categories as contingent and often oppressive.

This form of recognition translates to LGBTQ individuals in educational settings when the curriculum recognizes or makes intelligible past and present issues that affect the lives of LGBTQ individuals. The recognition of LGBTQ individuals is especially important in social studies education because LGBTQ individuals can transform our understandings of areas such as geography, economics, civics, and history. This is not to say that LGBTQ individuals are absent from these areas, but that they have been included without acknowledgement of their gender or sexual identities. Without this acknowledgement, students are left assuming that the geographies, economics, civics, and histories of LGBTQ individuals match the normative structures defined by patriarchal, cisgendered, and heteronormative discourses. This renders LGBTQ people unrecognizable, which poses a fundamental problem when education is aimed at preparing individuals to participate effectively in democratic communities. This type of critical democratic education increases the chances that students and educators will be better able to answer the question of *Who are you?*

An Ethics of Recognition

An ethics of recognition in curriculum and instruction would recognize the unique positionalities of students and educators. Queer theory helps in understanding how LGBTQ individuals are excluded or silenced in public schools. Heteronormativity functions to define and categorize heterosexuality and cisgender identities as 'normal'. This explains why LGBTQ individuals are excluded from instructional materials and classroom conversations. The symptoms and tools of this silence are transphobia, sexism, homophobia, and bullying. Because cisgender and heterosexual identities are the norm by which all else is measured in dominant discourses and society, those who are or appear to not fit into these discourses are deemed deficient or lacking. In a way, we are considered less than human, people to fear, fix, or in some circumstances assaulted. Butler (2006) writes:

> When we consider the ordinary ways that we think about humanization and dehumanization, we find the assumption that those who gain representation, especially self-representation, have a better chance of being humanized, and those who have no chance to represent themselves run a greater risk of being treated as less than human, regarded as less than human, or indeed, not regarded at all.
>
> (p. 141)

Dehumanization is the result of a lack of recognition. This dehumanization has been the cause of some of the most horrific actions against human beings ranging from genocide to slavery to segregation to inequitable learning environments to bullying to hate speech.

Judith Butler's (2006) ethics of recognition provides guidance to developing a queer ethics that is joined with critical democratic education in a way that recognizes individuals and uncovers the inequalities related to a lack of recognition. Illustrating the critical self-reflexivity involved in this process, Butler writes:

> For representation to convey the human, then, representation must not only fail, but it must *show* its failure. There is something unrepresentable that we nevertheless seek to represent, and that paradox must be retained in the representation we give.
>
> (p. 144, emphasis in the original)

The third spaces that such inquiry can open defy definition and are complicated, but it is in this defiance where multiple epistemologies, individuals, narratives, and perspectives can be recognized. The norms of standardization, accountability, and efficiency that govern schools work against opening third spaces in curriculum. However, an ethics of recognition can examine such norms and the ways that they perpetuate social inequalities and a lack of recognition.

Conclusion

I return to the voices that began this chapter as a way to tie third space and recognition together with critical democratic and queer theories. Sedgwick (2011) asks, "What if the most productive junctures weren't the ones where *everything means the same thing*" (p. 200, emphasis in the original)? Norms of standardization and related accountability produce discourses that govern what can and can't be said in the curriculum. These discourses produce an "offical knowledge" (Apple, 2000) where the knowledge in the curriculum is portrayed as 'neutral,' 'natural,' and 'commonsense'. This view ignores the ways that power and knowledge are connected. The networks of power relations within schools and society are anything but neutral, and the curriculum favors the knowledge of dominant groups. A critical democratic and queered curriculum works against the need to silence voices in the interest of 'effiency'. Instead, the curriculum should provide all students with the "ability to be multicontextual in the various frameworks and reason-giving activities in public spaces" (West, 2011, p. 93). Hall (2003) writes that "Queer theorization demands a broad acknowledgement of the need for continued discussion, for diversity in perspective and articulation, and for challenging and disruptive speech, even that which challenges and disrupts queer claims themselves" (p. 6). This is the context of possibilities for social justice and an ethics of recognition that fosters third spaces and critical democracy.

Based upon my illustrations in following chapters and the ways of understanding that I present in this chapter, I later discuss possibilities for increasing recognition, critical democratic education, and social justice in the curriculum. As a foreshadowing of the concluding chapter, I propose a curriculum that draws upon an ethics of recognition by examining intersectionality, power/knowledge, norms, discourses, and third spaces. I synthesize my illustrations from California and Utah and apply Young's (2000) process of increasing inclusion to my examination of curriculum. She recommends three steps: (1) *Greeting* opens an ethical relationship in which one person acknowledges the needs of another. Referring to greeting, Young writes, "A speaker announces her presence as ready to listen and take responsibility for her relationship to her interlocutors, at the same time that it announces her distance from the others, their irreducible particularity" (p. 59); (2) *Rhetoric* is the style of communication. Young writes, "One reason to bring the category of rhetoric explicitly into focus is to notice in a situation of political conflict how some people can be excluded from the public by dismissal of their style" (p. 70); (3) *Narrative* and situated knowledge help us recognize multiple epistemologies and perspectives from the unique lived experiences and positionalities of individuals. Young writes, "Storytelling is often an important bridge in such cases between the mute experience of being wronged and political arguments about justice" (p. 72). Attention to greeting, rhetoric, and narrative provides possibilities for third spaces where critical democracy and LGBTQ recognition can exist within subject areas such as economics, geography, history, and civics.

Notes

1 This use of categories is sometimes referred to as strategic essentialism (Spivak, 1996). Butler (2011) cautions against such a strategy, writing, "the necessity to mobilize the necessary error of identity (Spivak's term) will always be in tension with the democratic contestation of the term which works against its deployments in racist and misogynist discursive regimes" (p. 174).
2 For detailed history of these, see (Foucault, 1990, 2003; Hall, 2003; Sullivan, 2003).

References

Apple, M. W. (2000). *Official knowledge: Democratic education in a conservative age* (2nd ed.). New York: Routledge.

Apple, M. W. (2004). *Ideology and curriculum* (3rd ed.). New York: Routledge-Falmer.

Apple, M. W., & Beane, J. A. (Eds.). (2007). *Democratic schools: Lessons in powerful education* (2nd ed.). Portsmouth, NH: Heinemann.

Arent, H. (1958). *The human condition.* Chicago, IL: University of Chicago Press.

Benhabib, S. (1996). Toward a deliberative model of democratic legitimacy. In S. Benhabib (Ed.), *Democracy and difference: Contesting boundaries of the political* (pp. 67–94). Princeton, NJ: Princeton University Press.

Bhabha, H. K. (2009). In the cave of making: Thoughts on third space. In K. Ikas & G. Wagner (Eds.), *Communicating in the third space* (pp. ix–xiv). New York: Routledge.

Boler, M. (2004). All speech is not free: The ethics of "affirmative action pedagogy." In M. Boler (Ed.), *Democratic dialogue in education: Troubling speech, disturbing silence* (pp. 3–13). New York: Peter Lang.

Butler, J. (2006). *Precarious life: The powers of mourning and violence.* New York: Verso.

Butler, J. (2011). *Bodies that matter: On the discursive limits of sex (Kindle Edition).* New York: Routledge.

Butler, J. (2015). *Senses of the subject.* New York: Fordham University Press.

Camicia, S. P. (2007). Deliberating immigration policy: Locating instructional materials within global and multicultural perspectives. *Theory and Research in Social Education, 35*(1), 96–111.

Camicia, S. P. (2009). Identifying soft democratic education: Uncovering the range of civic and cultural choices in instructional materials. *The Social Studies, 100*(3), 136–142.

Camicia, S. P. (2012). An ethics of recognition in global and teacher education: Looking through queer and postcolonial Lenses. *International Journal of Development Education and Global Learning, 4*(1), 25–35.

Camicia, S. P. (2014). My pedagogical creed: Positionality, recognition, and dialogue in democratic education. In S. Totten (Ed.), *The importance of teaching social issues: Our pedagogical creeds* (pp. 166–175). New York: Routledge.

Camicia, S. P., & Bayon, A. (2012). Curriculum development collaboration between colonizer and colonized: Contradictions and possibilities for democratic education. In T. C. Mason & R. J. Helfenbein (Eds.), *Ethics and international curriculum work: The challenges of culture and context* (pp. 73–92). Charlotte, NC: Information Age.

Camicia, S. P., & Franklin, B. (2010). Curriculum reform in a globalised world: The discourses of cosmopolitanism and community. *London Review of Education, 8*(2), 93–104.

Camicia, S. P., & Zhu, J. (2011). Citizenship education under discourses of nationalism, globalization, and cosmopolitanism: Illustrations from China and the United States. *Frontiers of Education in China, 6*(4), 602–619.

Carlson, D. (1998). Who am I? Gay identitiy and a democratic politics of the self. In W. F. Pinar (Ed.), *Queer theory in education* (pp. 92–101). Mahwah, NJ: Lawrence Erlbaum Associates, Publishers.

Cohen, J. (1989). Deliberation and democratic legitimacy. In A. Hamlin & P. Pettit (Eds.), *The good polity: Normative analysis of the state* (pp. 17–47). Oxford, UK: B. Blackwell.

Collins, P. H. (2000). *Black feminist thought: Knowledge, consciousness, and the politics of empowerment.* New York: Routledge.

Delgado, R., & Stefancic, J. (2012). *Critical race theory: An introduction* (2nd ed.). New York: New York University Press.

Derrida, J. (1981). *Positions* (A. Bass, Trans.). Chicago, IL: University of Chicago Press.

Ferguson, R. A. (2013). The queer ethic and the spirit of normativity. In E. Haschemi Yekani, E. Kilian & B. Michaelis (Eds.), *Queer futures: Reconsidering ethics, activism, and the political* (pp. 165–176). Burlington, VT: Ashgate Publishing Company.

Foucault, M. (1990). *The history of sexuality: Volume I: An introduction* (R. Hurley, Trans.). New York: Vintage Books.

Foucault, M. (1995). *Discipline and punishment: The birth of the prison.* (A. Sheridan, Trans.). New York: Vintage Books.

Foucault, M. (2003). *Abnormal: Lectures at the Collège de France, 1974–1975* (G. Burchell, Trans.). New York: Picador.

Foucault, M. (2009). *History of Madness* (J. Murphy & J. Kahl, Trans.). New York: Routledge.

Habermas, J. (1994). Struggles for recognition in the democratic constitutional state (S. W. Nicholsen, Trans.). In C. Taylor & A. Gutmann (Eds.), *Multiculturalism: Examining the politics of recognition* (pp. 107–148). Princeton, NJ: Princeton University Press.

Habermas, J. (1996). *Between facts and norms: Contributions to a discourse theory of law and democracy* (W. Rehg, Trans.). Cambridge, MA: MIT Press.

Hall, D. E. (2003). *Queer theories.* New York: Palgrave Macmillan.

Hall, S. (2001). Foucualt: Power, knowlege, and discourse. In M. Wetherell, S. Taylor & S. J. Yates (Eds.), *Discourse theory and practice: A reader* (pp. 72–81). London: SAGE Publications.

Halperin, D. M. (1995). *Saint foucault: Towards a gay hagiography.* New York: Oxford University Press.

Haraway, D. (1988). Situated knowledges: The science question in feminism and the privilege of partial perspective. *Feminist Studies, 14*(3), 575–599.

Harding, S. (1993). *The "racial" economy of science: Toward a democratic future.* Bloomington, IN: Indiana University Press.

Haschemi Yekani, E., Kilian, E., & Michaelis, B. (2013). Introducing queer futures. In E. Haschemi Yekani, E. Kilian & B. Michaelis (Eds.), *Queer futures: Reconsidering ethics, activism, and the political* (pp. 1–15). Burlington, VT: Ashgate Publishing Company.

Klein, N. A., Markowitz, L. J., Puchner, L., & Anderson, J. K. (2011). Undressing the hidden curriculum: Sexuality education and middle school literature. In D. Carlson & D. L. Roseboro (Eds.), *The secuality curriculum and youth culture* (pp. 288–302). New York: Peter Lang Publishing, Inc.

Kosciw, J. G., Greytak, E. A., Palmer, N. A., & Boesen, M. J. (2014). *The 2013 national school climate survey: The experiences of lesbian, gay, bisexual and transgender youth in our nation's schools.* New York: GLSEN (Gay, Lesbian & Straight Education Network).

Kull, R. M., Kosciw, J. G., & Greytak, E. A. (2015). *From statehouse to schoolhouse: Anti-bullying policy efforts in the U.S. states and school districts.* New York: GLSEN (Gay, Lesbian & Straight Education Network).

Lapointe, A. A. (in press). Queering the social studies: Lessons to be learned from Canadian secondary school Gay-Straight Alliances. *The Journal of Social Studies Research.*

Mayo, J. B. (2013). Critical pedagogy enacted in the gay-straight alliance-new possibilities for a third space in teacher development. *Educational Researcher, 42*(5), 266–275.

Meyer, E. J. (2012). From here to queer: Mapping sexualities in education. In E. R. Meiners & Q. Therese (Eds.), *Sexualities in education: A reader* (pp. 9–17). New York: Peter Lang Publishing, Inc.

Pinar, W. F. (2011). *The character of curruiculum studies: Bildung, currere, and the recurring question of the subject.* New York: Palgrave Macmillan.

Russell, S. T., Muraco, A., Subramaniam, A., & Laub, C. (2009). Youth empowerment and high school Gay-Straight Alliances. *Journal of Youth and Adolescence, 38*(7), 891–903.

Russell, S. T., Toomey, R. B., Crockett, J., & Laub, C. (2010). LGBT politics, youth activisim, and civic engagement. In L. R. Sherrod, J. Torney-Purta & C. A. Flanagan (Eds.), *Handbook of research on civic engagement in youth* (pp. 471–494). Hoboken, NJ: John Wiley & Sons, Inc.

Sedgwick, E. K. (2011). *Weather in Proust.* Durham, NC: Duke University Press.

Snapp, S. D., Burdge, H., Licona, A. C., Moody, R. L., & Russell, S. T. (2015). Sudent's perspectives on LGBTQ-inclusive curriculum. *Equity & Excellence in Education, 48*(2), 249–265.

Snow, D. A. (2004). Framing processes, ideology, and discursive fields. In D. A. Snow, S. A. Soule & H. Kriesi (Eds.), *The Blackwell companion to social movements* (pp. 380–412). Malden, MA: Blackwell.

Soja, E. W. (2009). Toward a new consciousness of space and spatiality. In K. Ikas & G. Wagner (Eds.), *Communicating in the third space* (pp. 49–61). New York: Routledge.

Sokoll, T. (2013). Representations of trans youth in young adult literature: A report and a suggestion. *Young Adult Library Services, 11*(4), 23–26.

Spillman, L. (1995). Culture, social structures and discursive fields. *Current Perspectives in Social Theory, 15*, 129–154.

Spivak, G. C. (1996). Subaltern studies: Deconstructing historiography. In D. Landry & G. MacLean (Eds.), *The Spivak reader* (pp. 203–235). New York: Routledge.

Steinberg, M. W. (1999). The talk and back talk of collective action: A dialogic analysis of repertoires of discourse among Nineteenth-Century English cotton spinners. *The American Journal of Sociology, 105*(3), 736–780.

Sullivan, N. (2003). *A critical introduction to queer theory.* New York: New York University Press.

Weedon, C. (1999). *Feminism, theory and the politics of difference.* Malden, MA: Blackwell Publishers Inc.

West, C. (2011). Prophetic religion and the future of capitalist civilzation. In E. Mendieta & J. VanAntwerpen (Eds.), *The power of religion in the public sphere* (pp. 92–100). New York: Columbia University Press.

Young, I. M. (2000). *Inclusion and democracy.* New York: Oxford University Press.

3   LGBTQ Issues and
Utah Schools

The link between religion and politics is apparent in Utah. This has the effect of making one set of values and worldviews the point of departure and return for policies and resources. The Mormon Church and its followers are a dominant part of the state's population and influence most of the politics in the state. Policies governing everything from public behavior to schools are a reflection of the norms of the Mormon religion. In this chapter, I examine how these norms interact with inclusivity, exclusivity, and recognition related to school policies and curriculum around LGBTQ individuals. I first provide cases that illustrate the way that contexts affect the ways that LGBTQ individuals and issues are included or excluded from the curriculum. This is true with the official and unofficial curriculum. When I say the unofficial curriculum, I mean the events and learning that take place outside of the stated educational objectives and curriculum of the school, which can be inside or outside of the school. When applied to school settings, Apple (2004) calls this the hidden curriculum. Next, I include the reflections of three educators in the state who struggle with ways to increase LGBTQ inclusion in the curriculum.

Cases of Context

There is a reactionary climate in Utah that defines 'normal' in strict terms of patriarchal gender roles and sexual attractions. This translates into the privileging of male over female, heterosexual desire over homosexual desire, 'traditional families' over 'nontraditional families,' and cisgender individuals over transgender individuals. Conflicts inside and outside of schools illustrate the way this privileging maintains inequitable power relations by enforcing the norms of the dominant culture. Four cases illustrate these relations within the Utah context. They are related to teacher identity, Gay Straight Alliances, and prohibitions on LGBTQ books and research.

Within this context, Salt Lake City is often ranked as one of the best LGBTQ cities. For example, a 2016 article in *The Advocate* (Advocate Editors, 2016) ranked Salt Lake City as eighth in the queerest cites in America. *The Advocate* cites Salt Lake's LGBT film festivals and the election of Jackie Biskupski, the first openly gay mayor, as indications of the uniqueness of Utah's state capital. This was one of many such rankings that have placed Salt Lake City as LGBTQ inclusive. Whereas the criteria of these rankings are important and valuable, the topics of schools and school curriculum rarely figure into the equations for the rankings. In what follows in this chapter, I discuss some examples of the ways that LGBTQ issues, discourses, and perspectives are included and excluded from the official and unofficial curriculum.

Teacher Identity

LGBTQ teachers have a unique challenge within the context of a community that condemns individuals who are not recognized in relation to patriarchal and dominant views of gender identity and sexual orientation. This was apparent in the case of Wendy Weaver, who now goes by the name of Wendy Chandler (ACLU of Utah, 2003; Piatt, 2003; Williams, 2012). Over the course of her 17 years of teaching, Chandler had a record as an excellent teacher and girls' volleyball coach. After Chandler divorced her husband and started living with another woman, members of the community started to notice their relationship. Talk in the community increased when Chandler and her partner were seen holding hands in public.

A student asked Chandler whether she was a lesbian, and Chandler acknowledged that she was. A group of parents complained to the school district about Chandler being out to her students. As a result, the school placed a gag order on her, demanding that she not discuss her sexual orientation on or off campus. Chandler sought legal representation from the American Civil Liberties Union (ACLU) in order to defend herself against these restrictions. She successfully won her case against the gag order. However, a conservative group called the Eagle Forum filed suit against Chandler and the state board of education for not firing Chandler. In 2003, the Utah Supreme Court decided that avenues exist in the licensing of teachers that made it unnecessary for the courts to get involved with the case. Although Chandler was free from the charges and lawsuit, she had spent 5 years of her life defending herself against groundless charges and attacks.

Chandler was an excellent teacher and coach, but those who sought to harm her used her case as a way to enforce a patriarchy and heteronormativity. By making an example of her in this way, her critics sent a strong message to students, educators, and community members that teacher identity would be policed. The gag order that was first placed upon Chandler was an attempt to control what was included and excluded in the school curriculum. Teacher identity played an important role in control of the curriculum. It is difficult to say how this case influenced the way that LGBTQ teachers discussed their identities in schools, but the reaction to Chandler by the school and community could give LGBTQ teachers a reason for cautiousness. Thus, teacher identity is an aspect of the context for LGBTQ curriculum in Utah schools. The context of fear and policing is aligned with what some of the educators that I interviewed observed.

Gay-Straight (GSA) and Queer-Straight (QSA)[1] Alliance Clubs

In addition to providing LGBTQ-inclusive environments, GSAs and QSAs in Utah provide one of the most powerful illustrations of the context in which curriculum is experienced by students. The complicated conversation around curriculum involves what subjects are taught and what subjectivities are recognized. School administration and community resistance to the GSA clubs places the question of curriculum on center stage because most of the conflicts over GSAs involve a question of what counts as curricular and noncurricular. Although the first conflict over a GSA club occurred in 1995, school district policies that hinder the formation of GSAs continues to the present day (Van Valkenburg, 2013). Current attempts to deny such clubs fail in light of legal precedence; however, the attacks on such clubs send a powerful message about what knowledge, discourses, perspectives, voices, and subjectivities have equal access to educational settings.

One of the most well-known examples of LGBTQ curriculum struggles in Utah occurred just prior to the Wendy Chandler case. As with the Chandler case, East High School in Salt Lake City experienced the glare of a national spotlight as some in the community sought to ban support for LGBTQ students and their allies. In 1995, East High School students sought to form a GSA (Lambda Legal, 2013). Rather than allow the club, the school district attempted to satisfy The Equal Access Act (The Equal Access Act, 1984) by denying all clubs that were considered noncurricular. This extended to clubs with themes ranging from the "Polynesian Club to the Students Against Drunk Driving Club" (Brooke, 1996, paragraph 8). The litigation surrounding the case for allowing the GSA had far-reaching impact for the nation. According to Lambda Legal:

> This case more than any other put the issue of GSAs on the nation's radar, letting students know they could fight back and letting school districts know they might be in violation of the law. To increase the impact, Lambda Legal wrote the first-ever guidelines for students, parents and lawyers about the Equal Access Act and began a massive outreach effort to education and legal groups around the country.
>
> (paragraph 3)

Christian groups advocated for passage of The Equal Access Act because they wanted Christian clubs to be able to meet at schools. GSA supporters sought to change district policy around GSAs using the Equal Access Act, saying that GSAs were not granted the same access to school settings and resources as other clubs.

The act has been one of the key laws that GSA advocates use to support GSA clubs. Senator Orin Hatch from Utah sponsored the law. He expressed his dismay that the law was being used by GSAs to support their requests to meet at schools. As quoted by Brooke (1996), Hatch said, "The act was never intended to promulgate immoral speech or activity" (paragraph 7). It is clear from the remarks of Hatch and others that they intended to implement controls on speech and action surrounding schools and curriculum. One of the most outspoken groups against the GSA at East High was Gayle Ruzicka of the Utah Eagle Forum. She is quoted by Brooke as saying, "We are going to win this battle—and Utah will again be in the forefront . . . Homosexuals can't reproduce, so they recruit. And they are not going to use Utah high school and junior high school campuses to recruit" (paragraph 5). Norms that are defined by patriarchal, heterosexist, and cisgender power relations within and outside of schools governed this form of exclusion.

The litigation had a few phases and groups challenging the school policy. Those involved in the challenge were the "ACLU of Utah, along with cooperating attorneys Laura Milliken Gray and Marlin Criddle, the ACLU of Northern California, Lambda Legal Defense and Education Fund, and the National Center for Lesbian Rights" (American Civil Liberties Union, 2000, paragraph 3). The first suit claimed that the school had violated the 1984 Equal Access Act by allowing some noncurricular clubs to meet while not allowing LGBTQ-supportive clubs to meet. As such, the district violated the free speech rights of students and prohibited speech that was LGBTQ supportive. The judge agreed that the district had violated the 1984 Equal Access Act. In the second litigation,

GSA supporters appealed the first decision because they believed the first decision was too broad, leaving the school district with too much latitude to judge which clubs were curricular and which clubs were not. This could interfere with the free speech of clubs that the district did not deem curricular. In the appeal, multiple groups wrote amicus briefs. According to the ACLU:

> The Asian American Legal Defense and Education Fund, the Hispanic Bar Association of the District of Colombia, the National Asian Pacific American Legal Consortium, and the National Organization for Women Legal Defense and Education Fund also submitted an amicus brief in which they stressed that non-curricular clubs benefit all students, and that policies such as that adopted by the Salt Lake City School District are particularly damaging to minority students. (paragraph 6)

The school district's power to recognize what clubs are curricular and what clubs are not serves the interest of dominant groups who reinforce the norms of dominant cultures. In other words, the power of recognition that the school district claimed functioned to use the curriculum as a tool to maintain and increase the power of White, male, heterosexual, cisgender, and documented citizens.

The school district eventually withdrew its actions against the GSAs and other marginalized clubs. After two lawsuits, $174,550 in legal fees, student protests, media attention, and the possibility of $300,000 in additional legal fees, the school board decided to change its position on the clubs (Toomer-Cook, 2000). The process lasted for more than 5 years, but the impact was profound upon the community and nation. GSA supporters now had more tools to fight discriminatory curriculum and school practices.

During the course of the GSA case that started at East High, conservative and LGBTQ-inclusive groups gained support and framed their competing messages in the media. LGBTQ-supportive groups and their allies gained strength as a result of their resistance to public policies aimed at excluding and not recognizing them. Mayberry (2008) describes some of the ways that students engaged in activism and curriculum:

> Subsequent meetings were often devoted to discussions about the particular aspects of their school they would like to see changed, such as the elimination of homophobic jokes told in classrooms and ignored by teachers. In the process, they began to form clearer understandings of institutional heterosexism and began to develop

initial strategies of resistance. These did not emerge from the deficit discourse which often frames LGBT students as a "problem." Rather, these understandings and strategies came from students' awareness of and resistance to heterosexism, providing the foundation to engage in intentionally political activities to tackle the hidden curriculum of compulsory heterosexuality.

(pp. 23–24)

Based upon their examination of GSAs and youth civic engagement, Russell, Toomey, Crockett, and Laub (2010) found that student involvement in GSAs increased student sense of empowerment. They write,

Youth participation in GSA empowered them to feel more confident about their advocacy skills . . . 60% of youth responded that they strongly agree that "This year after doing things with my GSA, I feel more confident about fighting homophobia, transphobia, and other injustices."

(p. 486)

The case of East High provided an excellent illustration of how GSAs can increase the civic-mindedness and political activism of youth.

Unfortunately, the struggles of GSAs in Utah have continued 15 years after the East High victories. This has taken the form of new rules developed by the state that govern every aspect of club formation and operation, and the rules often work against GSAs (Johnson, 2007). The rules took effect in April 2007. The underlying intent of the law was revealed by State Senator D. Chris Buttars, who was quoted by Johnson as saying:

"If a gay-straight club wants to meet together, as they say they do, just for friendship, I have no problem with that," Mr. Buttars said. "But I think school districts should have the authority to do whatever they need to do [to] protect their schools—the law gives them authority to make decisions to protect the physical, emotional, psychological or moral well being of students.

(paragraph 7)

Two of the most harmful rules of the policy are that students must gain a parental signature to join a club and students must not discuss human sexuality. Given the dominance of the religious community that holds discriminatory views against LGBTQ individuals in Utah, the demand that parents give permission in order for students to attend a GSA is a significant barrier for the students who might most need the support of a GSA or the message that they send to the school community. LGBTQ students are ensnared within a cultural/religious context of prejudice and discrimination. In many instances, a student asking for permission would be an act of coming out to guardians who disagree with supporting their LGBTQ child because of the guardians' religious beliefs.

Although LGBTQ youth in Utah face obstacles in their efforts to build GSAs, the amount of clubs increases each year. According to Winters (2010), the number of clubs increased statewide from 10 in 2009 to 27 in 2010. Unfortunately, the battle over clubs still continues. As recently as 2013, Box Elder School District in Utah considered a proposal to ban all noncurricular clubs rather than allow a GSA at Box Elder High School (Van Valkenburg, 2013). Fortunately, the district and school eventually allowed the club to meet. The first meeting occurred in 2014 (Van Valkenburg, 2014). The Box Elder case illustrates that the struggle over GSAs is not over. This is especially true for the more conservative communities within Utah.

Book Banning

Recognition and LGBTQ inclusiveness has also been restricted in the types of books that students find on library shelves. A 2012 controversy erupted over a book written by Polacco (2009) entitled, *In Our Mothers' House*. The book was originally purchased by Windridge Elementary School because the book had "two mothers and librarians wanted to foster inclusion" (Rogers, 2012, paragraph 15). A parent with a student at Windridge Elementary School in Kaysville complained that her child had brought home a book that she found objectionable. In a letter to the school media committee, the parent wrote:

> My kindergarten student came home with this book. I felt it was inappropriate for her level. A book that discusses sexuality is best left in a public library, not a school, where children are accompanied by a parent to help them make book selections . . . It is trying to teach tolerance, through the topic of homosexuality. I believe tolerance is good to teach but this book came across as propaganda.
>
> (Wood, 2012, paragraphs 8–9)

The school media committee decided to move the book to a section of the school library where older students could have access to it. The mother appealed this decision to the school district, sending her letter and a petition containing 25 signatures. In response to the complaint and petition, the school district removed *In Our Mothers' House* (Polacco, 2009) from the shelves of libraries in five elementary schools (Wood, 2012). Students could still access the book, but they needed a note from their guardians giving them permission. This stipulation mirrors the requirement that school club members attain parental permission. This is problematic on multiple levels. The stipulation prevents access for students who will not ask for this type of permission if parents and the community communicate in a variety of ways that LGBTQ individuals are dangerous or abnormal. According to Rogers (2012) the "district's decision followed an April 30 meeting during which a seven-member committee determined the book isn't aligned with district curriculum standards" (paragraph 12). The district spokesman, Chris Williams, also said that the book was deemed to promote homosexuality, which is against state law. In addition, the committee said that the book was not age appropriate.

The decision to remove the book sent a message that same-sex relationships should not be recognized in any way by schools. Although the complaint was about a book in the school library and not the classroom, the committee's decision focused upon curriculum standards. The ban in classrooms was intensified by the controversy over a book that was not in classrooms but in libraries, where a greater degree of freedom of speech is expected. In the wake of the decision to remove *In Our Mothers' House* (Polacco, 2009), one of the district parents, Weston Clark, said in an interview that the decision "essentially put LGBT families behind the counter" (Rogers, 2012, paragraph 11). In response to the claims that the book was deemed by some to be inappropriate, Clark said, "What exactly do you find 'inappropriate' about my family? We're great citizens, we pay our taxes, we go to work, we keep up our yard" (paragraph 5). John Mejia, legal director of the ACLU of Utah said, "Taking a book off the shelves and hiding it behind a librarian's desk makes the book more difficult to read, and it sends the message that there is something wrong with the book and with children who have same-sex parents" (American Civil Liberties Union, 2012, paragraph 6).

Clark's experience and comments align with those of the author of *In Our Mothers' House.* Polacco (2012) explains an event that led to her writing of the book:

> One year I was visiting a fourth grade class and the teacher had arranged for me to hear essays that her students had written entitled: "My Family." I heard one after another and was moved by their perspectives and the love they held for their families. Then, one little girl stood up and began to read. She was immediately asked to take her seat by an aide. The aide said scornfully, "No dear . . . you don't come from a real family . . . sit down!" This child came from a family of two

mothers and two adopted siblings. I was so appalled and insulted on that child's behalf that I immediately, after school that day, went back to my hotel room and wrote, *In Our Mothers' House.*

(paragraphs 4–6)

Describing families as "inappropriate" or "not real" are harmful adjectives that serve to reinforce patriarchal and heteronormative structures within the curriculum. In *Obergefell et al. v. Hodges* (2015), the Supreme Court's decision for states to recognize same-sex marriage was partially based upon the reality of damage done to children when society does not recognize same-sex marriages. The Court wrote:

Without the recognition, stability, and predictability marriage offers, children suffer the stigma of knowing their families are somehow lesser. They also suffer the significant material costs of being raised by unmarried parents, relegated to a more difficult and uncertain family life. The marriage laws at issue thus harm and humiliate the children of same-sex couples.

(p. 3)

By placing *In Our Mothers' House* behind the library counter and off of the library shelves, the school was communicating to students and the community that the school did not recognize same-sex relationships as it did heterosexual relationships. This lack of recognition was an injustice that was central to the dispute.

The ACLU filed a complaint related to the case (*Weber v. Davis School District*, 2012). It claimed, among other points, that *In Our Mothers' House* was not part of instruction but in the school library. Afterward, Pamela Park (2013), an assistant superintendent, responded to the main complaint that the book violated school policy that instruction not advocate homosexuality. She wrote:

The Committee considered the applicability of Utah Code §53A-13–101, in deciding whether to remove or restrict access to In Our Mothers' House. The book has never been recommended or used as instructional material and therefore, the statute does not require removal or restriction of the book.

(paragraph 5)

Because the book was not part of instruction but in the school library, it could not be removed from the shelves on the basis that it advocated homosexuality. Although an important victory, the wording of the decision indicates that the outcome might have been different if the book were part of the classroom curriculum. One interpretation is that as a matter of free speech, the book is allowed in a school library, but same-sex relationships are still excluded from recognition or validation within the official curriculum.

Joshua Block, with the ACLU (American Civil Liberties Union, 2013), said of the decision,

> Children with same-sex parents shouldn't be made to feel like their families are something to be hidden away . . . Davis County schools include kids from all kinds of families, including ones like the family depicted in this book. We're glad the district recognizes this book's place is out on the shelves, not out of sight.
>
> (paragraph 9)

It is unfortunate that this recognition does not extend to the curriculum in classrooms.

In addition to the attempted prohibitions mentioned in the earlier cases, Utah has policy restrictions that almost prohibit research related to sexual orientation within schools. This prohibition is part of student privacy laws specific to Utah. Whereas on the surface the prohibition is supposed to protect students, the effect of the policy is to exclude marginalized student perspectives in research. This prohibition leaves social inequalities related to sexual orientation unexamined, as well as bolstering patriarchal and heteronormative systems of oppression. The cases in this section provide illustrations of the ways that exclusionary and inclusionary discourses function in and out of schools in Utah. Although there have been important resistances and victories against exclusion, there are significant constraints on inclusion.

Educator Reflections

As I mentioned in the introduction, I initially intended to visit schools in order to find examples of Utah teachers who create and implement LGBTQ-inclusive curriculum. Because of the laws within the state, this research was not possible. Even if such policies did not exist, finding such examples would be challenging because there is a general culture of fear within schools surrounding LGBTQ issues. As the illustrations in the prior sections indicate, although there have been important victories, educators who are willing to implement LGBTQ-inclusive curriculum take a risk that there will be community backlash. Whereas they might prevail in the long run, there is a good chance that conflicts will arise.

I interviewed three social studies educators who were nominated by others in the community as exemplary educators who could reflect upon their experiences with LGBTQ-inclusive curriculum within the Utah context. Due to the climate already mentioned, I interviewed these educators off school properties. We also decided to use pseudonyms and remove as much identifiable information as possible in order to protect their anonymity. The irony of not being able to identify or recognize them within a framework of inclusion and recognition is not lost on me. The themes that emerged from these interviews provide snapshots concerning the context of Utah and the types of inclusion that educators provide in such a restrictive environment. These reflections fall under the themes of constraints and possibilities.

Constraints

Robyn, a middle school teacher, described her experiences at meetings with other teachers who live in a climate of fear that they can lose their jobs if they discuss LGBTQ issues or come out at their schools. Regardless of what the laws do or do not say, there is a perception that a move toward more inclusion in the curriculum is risky. Whereas some believe that firing a teacher for creating inclusive curriculum or coming out would be politically reckless for a school, fear of retribution is real for teachers. Robyn observed, "I don't think it's about the law. I think it's about perceptions." Perceptions of surveillance, as well as some of the other factors mentioned in the cases earlier, provide powerful policing mechanisms. Teachers and students are silenced in this environment because there is a threat in the air. Dylan, a high school teacher, remarked, "Every kid is related to somebody gay now . . . it seems like it's time for them to be able to talk about that in school, and I don't think right now most teachers dare do that." The perceptions of threat were also palpable during my conversations with other community members about LGBTQ inclusion in Utah schools.

When asked about the possibility of providing language in Utah's curriculum standards that includes LGBTQ individuals and issues, all three teachers thought that it would help, but they were skeptical about the possibility that this would happen. Related to LGBTQ inclusion, Dylan said that such standards would make him more confident teaching in this area. He related an experience where parents did not want their children to learn about Islam:

> We teach about Islam, and here it is in the standards. Once you say here it is in the standards, the state standards, people are kind of like

"well, okay there it is in the state standards, yes indeed." But there are parents out there that don't want their children to learn about Islam. But once it's in the state standards teachers feel fine doing it.

The state standards gave him grounds for defending recognition within the curriculum. When asked about the possibility of LGBTQ-inclusive standards in Utah, Dylan replied:

I think it would never happen right now. I shouldn't say never happen. It couldn't happen right now. [If we teach anything] having to do with gay culture, gay society, gay rights, gay issues, there would be a backlash that would say no. We are not going to talk about this. I think it's kind of a stupid thing to be against because you have kindergarten children with two moms, two dads. Why would you not? We know there are people like that. We know there are kids like that so to say this is what a family is, this is what a definition of a family is, the pattern is absurd because it's clearly not the only definition of a family and nobody owns the definition.

Dylan's comments indicate a strong discourse of traditional family as the norm running through Utah schools and communities. When asked about the possibility of standards that encourage LGBT-inclusive curriculum, the discourse of family would undermine such a possibility any time in the near future. Also related to the potential impact of LGBTQ-inclusive standards, Andrew, a high school teacher, remarked:

The analogy to me here is evolution in science. Science teachers absolutely have evolution in their textbooks and in their core standards, and it's expected that that theory is a central theory of scientific inquiry and would be taught. Yet there are many teachers who self-censor even teaching evolution in science class. The same thing I think happens with a lot of teachers in Utah who know at least if they know any history of the Wendy Weaver issues and the kind of real political work that people have taken to make sure that teachers are protected. But in terms of free speech and obligation to be inclusive, even if people feel like there is at least an ability to talk about homosexuality or LGBT issues in general, that doesn't necessarily mean that they feel safe doing it or even if they feel protected, they may not make that choice. There is a lot of fear going on too, I think there is so much fear and I think that some of the fear is the backlash that you see. Some of the latest legislation that's trying to make sure that the people who are religiously opposed to the LGBT community and can deny them service in the restaurants. I'm like, are you serious?

Whereas the LGBTQ-inclusive policies and curriculum standards might help, the culture of fear that educators experience around inclusion might counteract these supports. It is well known that social studies teachers serve as gatekeepers for the curriculum (Thornton, 2005). As mentioned by California educators in the next chapter, even with the LGBTQ-inclusive standards and a progressive state legislature, communities vary in their views about LGBTQ individuals and issues. Many educators are silenced when they are in communities or schools where there might be a backlash.

Other constraints over inclusion involve the overwhelming demands placed upon classroom teachers. Discourses of standardization and accountability have fueled multiple sets of curriculum standards related to state and national expectations. As I mentioned in Chapter 1, there is a limited amount of time and resources related to curriculum and instruction. Educators have to make choices over what is included and excluded. When asked about the effect of curriculum standards related to LGBTQ-inclusive curriculum, Robyn replied somewhat ambivalently:

> I think that curriculum should reflect reality or the standards should reflect reality. And so long term do I think that it will have an impact as people feel like, "Oh it's on paper therefore, maybe I should feel comfortable talking about it." Ya, I think so. Do I personally ever look at the standards to see which names are mentioned? No. I just don't. It's a laundry list of stuff I think. I'm biased, but in social studies, I don't think anyone ever actually expects that you are going to teach it all. In math, all the math teachers I know get stressed out if they don't make it through the standards, which makes me think that it might be slightly more realistic. Because when I look at the standards, it's like "Teach the whole history of the world in a semester." And it's usually pretty Eurocentric. And for those reasons, it's way too broad and focuses on stuff that doesn't necessarily relate to my students. I don't really pay any attention to it to be honest.

Although Robyn believed that inclusion within standards are good in that they would better "reflect reality" as well as relating better to students, the seemingly unrealistic "laundry list of stuff" is unreasonable. In the next section, I discuss how educators are framing the curriculum in ways that recognize students. These comments, in combination with the comments of California educators in the next chapter, provide guidance surrounding curriculum design and implementation that is more critical, inclusive, democratic, and socially just.

Opportunities

Recognition was prevalent in teacher reflections upon opportunities for more inclusive curriculum. The teachers moved away from an additive approach, which was one of the aspects of standards that Robyn found unrealistic due to the volume of knowledge added. The additive approach has been common in curriculum reform aimed toward inclusion (Banks, 1994; Zimmerman, 2002). This has been at the expense of more transformative approaches that question the dominant narratives and assumptions in the curriculum. By moving toward a transformative approach, the pressures from the additive approach are alleviated because recognition is braided into themes such as the relationship of norms to power/ knowledge and social injustices. These themes can guide student inquiry in a more resourceful manner because different subject areas overlap in content. Robyn described a transformative approach:

> I teach geopolitics and I teach history. I've taught a bunch of different subjects over the years. Social studies things. And my philosophy is just to treat it like it's just one other aspect of what we talk about. So whether it's our unit on race, class, and gender, we sort and break down terminology the kids need to know, or whether it's talking about human trafficking and talking about what is it . . . Why does that happen? What are our assumptions about girls and how they should be treated and you know all these things. Then when it comes up that also little boys are human trafficked and used in different ways. I mean, it's just kind of sadly normal and we just talk about those things. So I wouldn't say that I go out of my way to be like "Ok, I'm going to make sure to have . . . when we learn about the Renaissance, to like make sure we're talking about at least one gay person."

By discussing norms related to social injustices, Robyn moves away from an additive approach toward discussions about power, socially constructed oppressions, and the discourses that maintain them. This lens works towards recognition by examining the underlying structures that cause inequalities. Whether geography, history, civics, economics, or current events, this principle of transformation works across the curriculum. Andrew also referred to a transformative approach:

For me it's like saying to whole groups of people who have been disenfranchised over the years in the public school system, okay, look, . . . we need the Latino community and the refugee population and EL learners and the special ed kids and the gay kids and we need all of those communities to see themselves reflected in the curriculum. To see the stories of these people especially social studies brought before in a way that says, look, we have always been here, we have always been here, guess what? Surprise surprise! But it's high time, if we are serious about student achievement and about kids not dropping out and kids not feeling that they do not belong and kids saying none of this makes any difference to me, then we have an obligation to be thinking about how to make these things more inclusive.

One of the central ways to transform the curriculum is to question dominant narratives that have and continue to oppress marginalized individuals and groups. By recognizing different perspectives on schooling and society, students are able to engage social studies content on a different level that examines the link between power/knowledge and identities. This approach is not additive but transformative of the taken-for-granted narratives and discourses in curriculum. Robyn described how identity and positionality serve as other transformative themes that span the social studies curriculum:

In no matter what I'm teaching because, it one, lays the foundation for what kind of teacher I am and the kind of thinking I want kids to be doing; and two, I think it really relates whether [you're] learning history or geography to be thinking about how do we classify ourselves and others. So at the beginning of the year, often I start with a "Where I'm from poem." I don't know if you've heard of that but it's based off of a poem that some other person wrote and in it, it's just all these stanzas like "I'm from the roots of the tree that grew behind the porch. I'm from my grandmother's beef stew. I'm from, whatever . . . " So to do that, we'll often brainstorm parts of our identity, and I always model myself . . . And so that's one way that I sort of just start it, but then in the whole unit in that case we talk about race and what does it mean for something to be socially constructed? What is a chosen identity vs. an assigned identity? And then we take that and we talk about gender and we talk about the difference between gender expression and gender identity . . . and how those people think they go together but really don't necessarily. And we look at examples of people . . . But I may have mentioned this to you, but I have this awesome article about the Albanian women who live as men, historically and a few still today. And there was an article in the *New York Times* a few years ago about it. And so often I use that as my first foray into it to see how kids react because it's not at all about sexual orientation in theory. It's just like a need that the community had because of their expectations about what men could do in the society. And so it really messes with kids' heads and I think . . . I would like to think that the fact that I treated it as just like one more thing that we study helps. And then always . . . throughout all of it, I can get a read on where kids are at, which then kind of helps me know what I'm working with. And I will say every year it's more and more clear to me that no kids care.

Robyn described her work on identities, positionalities, and discourses as an organizing principle across the various social studies disciplines she teaches, as well as an overarching structure of each course. Throughout the semester, she and the students return to discussions of norms, identities, and social inequalities. These are bound by the concept of power/ knowledge as it is reflected in her focus upon the socially constructed nature of knowledge. The types of transformative curriculum that the Utah educators described opens a third space in the social studies curriculum where new possibilities arise for understanding individuals, communities, and social justice.

Conclusion

In the process of planning this research project, some pointed to the East High victory as a sign that Utah was more progressive than most might think in the area of LGBTQ inclusiveness. Although the case of East High was an important victory for students and communities in Utah and beyond, three things must be noted. First, consider the time period in which the cases in this chapter are reported. The struggles over the curriculum happened relatively late compared with more progressive states. The struggles have been fairly recent, and as descried by the teachers, the fear over conflict and retaliation continues to hinder inclusion, recognition, and curriculum transformation. Second, the influence of patriarchy and religion are extremely powerful. Educational policies in Utah have controlled what kinds of identities teachers can have, what associations students can form, what books students can read, and what the outside world can know about the experiences of marginalized students through research. Given this entire context, it is not surprising that Utah curriculum standards contain little recognition of LGBTQ individuals.

However, as the teachers who I spoke with illustrate, even within this restrictive environment, teachers have developed ways to resist inequitable schools and school policies. As gatekeepers, teachers can introduce transformative themes across their social studies curriculum. By focusing upon themes such as identities and inequality, power/knowledge, and norms, students can examine geography, history, civics, and economics in ways that increase recognition. Through this recognition, social inequalities can be seen through the light of critical democratic education.

Note

1 In Utah, GSAs are currently referred to as QSAs. For clarity, I have used the term GSA throughout.

References

ACLU of Utah. (2003, April 9). *Citzens of Nebo School District v. Weaver.* Retrieved from http://www.acluutah.org/legal-work/resolved-cases/item/189-citizens-of-nebo-school-district-v-weaver

Advocate Editors. (2016, February/March). Queerest cities in America. *The Advocate*, (1083), 46–53.

American Civil Liberties Union. (2000). East high Gay/Straight Alliance v. board of education and east high school PRISM club v. Cynthia L. Seidel (1999). Retrieved from http://www.acluutah.org/legal-work/resolved-cases/item/206-east-high-gay-straight-alliance-v-board-of-education-and-east-high-school-prism-club-v-cynthia-l-seidel

American Civil Liberties Union. (2012). Utah school district sued for removing children's book about lesbian parents from library. Retrieved from https://http://www.aclu.org/news/utah-school-district-sued-removing-childrens-book-about-lesbian-parents-library?redirect=lgbt-rights/utah-school-district-sued-removing-childrens-book-about-lesbian-parents-library

American Civil Liberties Union. (2013). Davis school district returns children's book about lesbian parents to library shelves. Retrieved from https://http://www.aclu.org/news/davis-school-district-returns-childrens-book-about-lesbian-parents-library-shelves?redirect=lgbt-rights/davis-school-district-returns-childrens-book-about-lesbian-parents-library-shelves

Apple, M. W. (2004). *Ideology and curriculum* (3rd ed.). New York: Routledge-Falmer.

Banks, J. A. (1994). Transforming the mainstream curriculum. *Educational Leadership*, *51*(8), 4–8.

Brooke, J. (1996, February 28). To be young, gay and going to high school in Utah. *The New York Times*. Retrieved from http://www.nytimes.com/1996/02/28/us/to-be-young-gay-and-going-to-high-school-in-utah.html

The Equal Access Act, 20 U.S.C., § 4071 Stat. (1984 August 11).

Johnson, K. (2007, March 17). Utah sets rigourous rules for school clubs, and gay ones may be target. *The New York Times*. Retrieved from http://www.nytimes.com/2007/03/17/education/17utah.html?_r=1&

Lambda Legal. (2013). East high Gay Straight Alliance v. board of education of Salt Lake city school district. Retrieved from http://www.lambdalegal.org/in-court/cases/east-high-gsa-v-board-of-ed-salt-lake

Mayberry, M. (2008). The story of a Salt Lake City gay-straight alliance: Identity work and LGBT youth. *Journal of Gay & Lesbian Issues in Education*, *4*(1), 13–31.

Obergefell et al. v. Hodges No. 576 U.S. (Supreme Court of the United States 2015).

Park, P. S. (2013, January 11). Davis school district letter about book [In our mothers' house] revised request for reconsideration opinion. Farmington, UT.

Piatt, R. (2003, April 4). Court rules in favor of lesbian teacher. Retrieved from http://www.ksl.com/?nid=148&sid=91264

Polacco, P. (2009). *In our mothers' house*. New York: Philomen Books.

Polacco, P. (2012, October 5). Not a real family? Book about two moms banned in Utah school district. Retrieved from https://http://www.aclu.org/blog/not-real-family-book-about-two-moms-banned-utah-school-district

Rogers, M. (2012, June 18). In wake of controversy, LGBT families to attend board meeting. *Salt Lake Tribune*. Retrieved from http://www.sltrib.com/sltrib/news/54326040–78/district-book-fa

Russell, S. T., Toomey, R. B., Crockett, J., & Laub, C. (2010). LGBT politics, youth activisim, and civic engagement. In L. R. Sherrod, J. Torney-Purta & C. A. Flanagan (Eds.), *Handbook of research on civic engagement in youth* (pp. 471–494). Hoboken, NJ: John Wiley & Sons, Inc.

Thornton, S. J. (2005). *Teaching social studies that matter: Curriculum for active learning*. New York: Teachers College Press.

Toomer-Cook, J. (2000, August 14). S.L. school board mulls club policy. *Deseret News*. Retrieved from http://www.deseretnews.com/article/777154/SL-school-board-mulls-club-policy.html

Van Valkenburg, N. (2013, November 11). Box elder teen sisters push for gay straight alliance club. *Standard Examiner*. Retrieved from http://www.standard.net/Local/2013/11/11/Box-Elder-teen-sisters-push-for-Gay-Straight-Alliance-club.html

Van Valkenburg, N. (2014, February 8). Box elder high gay-straight alliance club begins. *Standard Examiner*. Retrieved from http://www.standard.net/Local/2014/02/09/Box-Elder-High-gay-straight-alliance-club-begins

Weber v. Davis School District (United States District Court of Utah Northern Division 2012).

Williams, B. (2012). An accidental activist. Retrieved from http://gaysaltlake.com/news/2012/03/14/an-accidental-activist/

Winters, R. (2010, December 20). Gay student clubs blossoming in Utah. *The Salt Lake Tribune*. Retrieved from http://www.sltrib.com/sltrib/home/50845394–76/gay-clubs-utah-county.html.csp

Wood, B. (2012, June 19). Petition sheds light on parental concerns in same-gender book ban controversy. *Deseret News*. Retrieved from http://www.deseretnews.com/article/865557808/Petition-sheds-light-on-parental-concerns-in-same-gender-book-ban-controversy.html

Zimmerman, J. (2002). *Whose America?: Culture wars in the public schools.* Cambridge, MA: Harvard University Press.

4 LGBTQ Issues and California Schools

As one of the centers of LGBTQ culture and rights movements (Eaklor, 2008; Hirshman, 2012), California has been one of the most influential regions in framing LGBTQ issues. This is particularly true in relation to schools (Biegel, 2010; Cianciotto & Cahill, 2012; Miceli, 2005). This chapter mirrors the structure of the last chapter on Utah. I describe some important events that provide the cultural and political context in which the public school curriculum is embedded. The policies outside of schools provide a context for understanding how students and educators might include or exclude LGBTQ perspectives in the curriculum. Next, I include the insights of educators within the state that work toward LGBTQ inclusion.

Cases of Context

There is a progressive political climate in California that frames many of the LGBTQ issues in schools. Although strong regional differences exist, as evidenced in voting patterns from the coastal compared with valley regions, overall, California politics are progressive compared with most states. This is not to say that patriarchal gender and sexual identities don't govern the normalizing forces in the state, but it is to say that these forces interact with the resistances of progressive politics that support recognition. Four cases illustrate these resistances: the Briggs Initiative, large-scale school programs supporting LGBTQ youth, policies protecting LGBTQ students, The FAIR Act, and curriculum standards.

The Briggs Initiative

Within the context of curriculum, the 1978 Briggs Initiative (California Proposition 6) was an early indication of how unique the cultural and political context of California was in comparison to other regions of the country. The Briggs Initiative sought to bar gay and lesbian teachers from public schools (Adams, 2013). The initiative also barred anyone from teaching about homosexuality in schools "in a positive way" (Eaklor, 2008, p. 170). The following is wording from the initiative:

School Employees—Homosexuality. Initiative Statute

Provides for filing charges against schoolteachers, teacher's aides, school administrators or counselors for advocating, soliciting, imposing, encouraging or promoting private or public sexual acts defined in sections 286(a) and 288a(a) of the Penal Code between persons of same sex in a manner likely to come to the attention of other employees or students.

(School Employees—Homosexuality
California Initiative 160, 1977, p. 4)

Voters defeated the initiative 59 to 41 percent (Biegel, 2010; School Employees—Homosexuality California Initiative 160, 1977). This was an indication that the political and cultural context of California was unique in relationship to issues of same-sex attraction and curriculum because it was one of the few areas of the country where there was an explicit positive vote related to recognition in the curriculum. Positive viewpoints on same-sex relationships were not barred from schools, and school employees could not be fired because of their sexual orientation. Whereas the vote did not mean that recognition was required, it was significant in that recognition was not prohibited. The date of the vote is also significant and indicates an important part of the climate in California in 1977. The previous chapter cited current policies in Utah that prohibit same-sex recognition in the curriculum, as well as restrictions on research about sexual orientation in schools without parental permission. This 40-year lag between the two states is significant.

School Organizations

California is noted as one of the earliest states to implement sizable programs that support LGBTQ youth. Virginia Uribe started PROJECT 10 in 1985 in response to the case of a Black gay student named "Chris H." Chris was forced to leave his home at age 14 when he came out as gay. The school system also abandoned him. At multiple schools, other students verbally and physically assaulted Chris. School administration routinely responded to conflicts between Chris and other students by reprimanding Chris and eventually transferring him to another school. In effect, school administrations were placing the blame for violence upon Chris for not being straight. Rather than address the systemic inequalities that caused the violence, they placed the blame on him for not fitting in with their norm. Chris ended up dropping out of school.

A group of students approached Uribe and had similar stories to that of Chris. Uribe helped them begin a support group for students in similar situations and their allies (Miceli, 2005). In response to their investigation into Chris's case, the school administration also asked Uribe to develop a "model program to work with self-identified gay, lesbian, and bisexual youngsters in the school setting" (Uribe & Harbeck, 1992, p. 11). Research into the project showed positive results, and the Los Angeles Unified School District expanded the project to include all high schools in the district. The PROJECT 10 example is significant because it was the first LGBTQ-inclusive project of its scale within the nation. According to Miceli's (2005) research, PROJECT 10 "was the first ever in-school support group offered to LGBT students at a public high school" (p. 21). PROJECT 10 and the support materials predated the first official Gay-Straight Alliance (GSA).

The Gay-Straight Alliance Network is headquartered in San Francisco where it began with 40 GSA clubs in the San Francisco Bay Area. Since its founding by Carolyn Laub in 1998, the clubs now number over 900 (GSA Network, 2015b). The GSA Network became a national organization by 2005. The GSA Network of California has been instrumental in increasing the number of GSAs nationally. According to the GSA Network, 61 percent of public high schools in California have a GSA. The clubs provide places where students can support each other in their recognition of a range of sexual and gender identities. The GSA Network provides materials and trainings that support student organizations in their efforts to create safer school environments and LGBTQ-supportive policies.

Miceli (2005) writes, "From the start, the GSA Network made it an explicit goal to build coalitions, not only among LGBT and straight students, but also among students of different classes, races, and ethnicities" (p. 35). This is apparent in the literature from the organization and the research projects that the organization has conducted to support LGBT youth. Support materials for clubs indicate this on a section of their website, which advises upon ways to make GSAs more inclusive. It reads:

> The LGBTQ youth movement cannot survive unless it includes people of color and addresses issues of sexism, racism, classism, ageism, and environmental injustice. We must link ourselves together to

create a multi issue social justice movement which incorporates the needs and rights of multiple communities.

(GSA Network, 2015a)

This focus upon the recognition and positionalities of students provides an illustration of how the curriculum might increase recognition. Coalitions of different groups have the ability to examine social injustices and create social action that is inclusive. In addition, coalitions such as this can share strategies. Historically, this has been the way most successful social movements function (Snow, 2004; Tarrow, 1998; Tilly, 2004).

In addition, the GSA Network has been influential in advocating for the successful passage of 11 laws that protect students (GSA Network, 2015b, 2015c). The California Safety and Violence and Prevention Act of 2000 established that "all students and staff in public education facilities have the same right to a safe learning environment, regardless of their sexual orientation or gender identity" (p. 4). This landmark law provided the grounds for other laws that were to follow. In 2013, the passage of AB-1266 Pupil rights: Sex-segregated school programs and activities added protections in schools for transgender students. The law states that students be "permitted to participate in sex-segregated school programs and activities, including athletic teams and competitions, and use facilities consistent with his or her gender identity, irrespective of the gender listed on the pupil's records" (Pupil rights: Sex-segregated school programs and activities, 2013, p. 87). These policies create the legal context where school policies can recognize and support LGBTQ students.

Finally, multiple research projects have been supported and written by the GSA Network. These reports cover a range of topics from school climate to school policies. Research on LGBTQ-inclusive curriculum found that that:

> Students who reported any mention of LGBTQ people/issues in a classroom setting were also more likely to report feeling safe at school. Furthermore, students are even more likely to report positive outcomes regarding school safety when LGBTQ-inclusive lessons are described as "mostly supportive" as opposed to "neutral/mixed," or "mostly not supportive."

(Burdge, Sinclair, Laub, & Russell, 2012)

This work, in conjunction with other reports such as those from Gay, Lesbian & Straight Education Network (GLSEN) (Kosciw, Greytak,

Palmer, & Boesen, 2014; Kull, Kosciw, & Greytak, 2015), illustrate ways that schools influence the lives of LGBTQ youth either negatively or positively. This evidence, along with other sources of evidence, provides a compelling rationale for creating safe schools that value inclusive curriculum.

Fair, Accurate, Inclusive, and Respectful (FAIR) Education Act

The GSA Network has also been influential in changing school policies related to the LGBTQ content in instructional materials. In 2011, the California legislators signed into law the Fair, Accurate, Inclusive, and Respectful (FAIR) Education Act, SB 48, which, in part, requires that public school curriculum include lessons about the contributions of LGBTQ individuals to society. Referring to SB 48, the following is text from the California Department of Education website:

> The law made several additions to the *Education Code* sections dealing with the course of study, classroom instruction, and instructional materials. The bill added language to *Education Code* Section 51204.5, which prescribes the inclusion of the contributions of various groups in the history of California and the United States. This section already included men and women and numerous ethnic groups; the expanded language now includes (additions bolded):
>
> " . . . a study of the role and contributions of both men and women, Native Americans, African Americans, Mexican **Americans**, Asian **Americans**, Pacific Islanders, **European Americans, lesbian, gay, bisexual, and transgender Americans, persons with disabilities**, and members of other ethnic **and cultural** groups, to the economic, political, and social development of California and the United States of America, with particular emphasis on portraying the role of these groups in contemporary society."
>
> The legislation also added some requirements with regard to instructional materials. *Education Code* Section 51501 outlines prohibitions on material included in textbooks or other instructional materials. This section already included prohibitions on matter "reflecting adversely upon persons because of their race, sex, color, creed, handicap, national origin, or ancestry"; this bill added "sexual orientation" to the list. *Education Code* Section 60044 includes a similar prohibition; the language was added there as well, along with a prohibition on materials that contain materials that reflect adversely on persons on the basis of their occupation. *Education Code* Section

60040 directs governing boards to only adopt instructional materials that "accurately portray the cultural and racial diversity of our society." That section already included a number of groups, and was amended to include all of those in Section 51204.5 as listed above. Finally, the legislation provides a reminder to charter and alternative schools that they are also prohibited in engaging in discrimination per Section 235 of the *Education Code.*

(California Department of Education, 2011)

The changes in the code place California as a state leader in LGBTQ-inclusive curriculum policy and standards. The following are excerpts from a draft of the new curriculum standards framework. The draft is still being revised, but I provide excerpts throughout the rest of this section to illustrate the types of changes in the standards. The following is from grade two:

How do families remember their past? Students engage in the study [of] the history of a family and may construct a history of their own family, a relative's or neighbor's family, or a family from books. Through studying the stories of a very diverse collection of families, such as immigrant families, families with lesbian, gay, bisexual, or transgender parents and their children, families of color, step- and blended families, families headed by single parents, extended families, families with disabled members, families from different religious traditions, and adoptive families, students can both locate themselves and their own families in history and learn about the lives and historical struggles of their peers. In developing these activities, teachers should not assume any particular family structure and ask questions in a way that will easily include children from diverse family backgrounds. They need [to] be sensitive to family diversity and privacy, and to protect the wishes of students and parents who prefer not to participate.

(California Department of Education, 2015, p. 61)

The following excerpts are from grade four:

- Students can also study the famous court case *Mendez v. Westminster* (1947), predecessor to *Brown v. Board of Education* (1954) that banned the segregation of Mexican students; student activism at San Francisco State University and UC Berkeley in the 1960s that forced the recognition of Asian American identity and history; the occupation of Alcatraz by California Indians in 1969–1971; and the emergence of the nation's first gay rights organizations in the 1950s. In the 1970s, California gay rights groups fought for the right of gay men and women to teach, and, in the 2000s, for their right to get married, culminating in the 2013 and 2015 U.S. Supreme Court decisions *Hollingsworth v. Perry* and *Obergefell v. Hodges* (California Department of Education, 2015, pp. 114–115).

- They learn about the contributions of immigrants to California from across the country and globe, such as Dalip Singh Saund, an Indian Sikh immigrant from the Punjab region of South Asia who in 1957 became the first Asian American to serve in the U.S. Congress, Civil Rights activists Cesar Chavez and Dolores Huerta, Tech titans Sergey Brin (Google), and Jerry Yang (Yahoo), and Harvey Milk, a New Yorker who was elected to the San Francisco Board of Supervisors in 1977 as California's first openly gay public official (California Department of Education, 2015, pp. 115–116).

These excerpts from grades two and four illustrate the way that inclusiveness can be woven into the existing scope and sequence in all states. This is aligned with the expanding horizon model of curriculum where students in elementary grades increase the scale of their investigations as they proceed through the different grade levels. In the previous excerpt, students learn about the scale of families in the second grade and the state in fourth grade. These topics provide an indication of the ways that teachers can fashion elementary school curriculum to be more inclusive and transformative. Multiple opportunities exist for teachers to create curriculum that focuses upon norms, identities, power/knowledge, discourses, and social justice. The scale of the inquiries can change from grade to grade, but areas where LGBTQ individuals have been excluded from the elementary-level curriculum can be included in areas such as geography, history, economics, and civics.

The following are excerpts from the grade 11 draft of standards framework that illustrate some of the ways that inclusion at the secondary level might be achieved:

- LGBT life expanded in 1920s Harlem. At drag balls, rent parties, and speakeasies, rules about acceptable gendered behavior seemed more flexible for black and white Americans than in other parts of society, and many leading figures in the "Renaissance" such as Hughes, Locke, Cullen, and Rainey were lesbian, gay, or bisexual. The Harlem Renaissance led many African Americans to embrace a new sense of black pride and identity, as did Marcus Garvey, the Black Nationalist leader of a "Back to Africa" movement that peaked during this period (California Department of Education, 2015, pp. 524–525).

- Students learn about the roles and sacrifices of American soldiers during the war, including the contributions of the Tuskegee Airmen, the 442nd Regimental Combat team, women and gay people in military service, the Navajo Code Talkers, and the important role played by Filipino soldiers in the war effort (California Department of Education, 2015, p. 537).

- Military officials established an unprecedented effort to screen out and reject homosexuals, although gay men and lesbians still served in the armed forces in significant numbers. Some found toleration in the interests of the war effort, but many others were imprisoned or dishonorably discharged. That persecution set the stage for increased postwar oppression and organized resistance (California Department of Education, 2015, p. 542).

- . . . the term "McCarthyism" signifies the entire era of suspicion and disloyalty. Hysteria over national security extended to homosexuals, considered vulnerable to blackmail and thus likely to reveal national secrets. The public Red Scare overlapped with a Lavender Scare. Congress held closed-door hearings on the threat posed by homosexuals in sensitive government positions. A systematic investigation, interrogation, and firing of thousands of suspected gay men and lesbians from federal government positions extended into surveillance and persecution of suspected lesbians and gay men in state and local government, education, and private industry. Students can debate whether such actions served national security and public interests and consider how the Lavender Scare shaped attitudes and policies related to lesbian, gay, bisexual, and transgender people from the 1950s to the present (California Department of Education, 2015, p. 550).

- They recognize the leadership of the black churches, female leaders such as Rosa Parks, Ella Baker, and Fannie Lou Hamer, and gay leaders such as Bayard Rustin, all of whom played key roles in shaping the movement. Through the careful selection and analysis of the many primary sources available from the period, students come to understand both the extraordinary courage of ordinary black men, women, and children and the interracial character of the civil rights movement (California Department of Education, 2015, p. 559).

- The advances of the black civil rights movement encouraged other groups—including women, Hispanics and Latinos, American Indians, Asian Americans, Pacific Islanders, gay, lesbian, bisexual, and transgendered Americans, students, and people with disabilities—to mount their own campaigns for legislative and judicial recognition of their civil equality. Students can use the question **How did various movements for equality build upon one another?** (California Department of Education, 2015, pp. 561–562).

- On the social and cultural front, feminists tackled day-to-day sexism with the mantra, "The personal is political." Many lesbians active in the feminist movement developed lesbian feminism as a political and cultural reaction to the limits of the gay movement and mainstream feminism to address their concerns (California Department of Education, 2015, p. 564).

- Students also examine the emergence of a movement for lesbian, gay, bisexual, and transgender rights starting in the 1950s with California-based groups like the Mattachine Society and the Daughters of Bilitis. Throughout the 1950s and early 1960s, these fairly secretive organizations created support networks; secured rights of expression and assembly; and cultivated relationships with clergy, doctors, and legislators to challenge teachings and laws that condemned homosexuality as sinful, sick, and/or criminal. In the 1960s, younger activists, often poorer and sometimes transgender, began to confront police when they raided gay bars and cafes in Los Angeles, San Francisco, and most famously at the Stonewall Inn in New York City in 1969. Organizations such as the Gay Liberation Front and the Gay Activists Alliance called on people in the movement to "come out" as a personal and political act. Students can consider figures such as Alfred Kinsey, Harry Hay, Jose Sarria, Del Martin and Phyllis Lyon, Frank Kameny, Sylvia Rivera, and Harvey Milk. By the mid-1970s, LGBT mobilization led to successes: the American Psychiatric Association stopped diagnosing homosexuality as a mental illness; 17 states had repealed laws criminalizing gay sexual behavior; 36 cities had passed laws banning antigay discrimination; and gay-identified neighborhoods had emerged in major cities. Students can consider how a 1958 Supreme Court decision that rejected the Post Office's refusal to distribute a gay and lesbian magazine through U.S. mails (*One, Inc. v. Olsen*), and a 1967 Supreme Court decision that upheld the exclusion and deportation of gay and lesbian immigrants (*Boutilier v. Immigration and Naturalization Service*) relate to more recent decisions, such as the 1986 decision that upheld state sodomy laws (*Bowers v. Hardwick*), the 2003 decision overturning such laws (*Lawrence v. Texas*), 2013 and 2015 decisions on same-sex marriage (*United States v. Windsor*, *Hollingsworth v. Perry*, and *Obergefell v. Hodges*), and the constitutional guarantee of equal protection under the law for transgender individuals, as exemplified through successful claims of employment discrimination including *Glenn v. Brumby, Schroer v. Billington*, and the Equal Employment Opportunity Commission's decision in *Macy v. Holder* (California Department of Education, 2015, pp. 564–565).

- In what ways have issues such as education; civil rights for people of color, immigrants, and lesbian, gay, bisexual, and transgender Americans, and disabled Americans; economic policy; the environment; and the status of women remained unchanged over time? In what ways have they changed? (California Department of Education, 2015, p. 569)

- **In what ways have issues such as education; civil rights for people of color, immigrants, and lesbian, gay, bisexual, and transgender Americans, and disabled Americans; economic policy; the environment; and the status of women remained unchanged over time? In what ways have they changed?** The growth of the lesbian, gay, bisexual, and transgender rights movement, for example, led to the pioneering role of gay politicians such as Elaine Noble, who was elected to the Massachusetts House of Representatives in 1974, and Harvey Milk, elected in 1977 to the San Francisco Board of Supervisors. Students can learn about how such activism informed the history of the AIDS epidemic in the United States. California students are particularly poised to tap local history resources on the epidemic related to a retreat from some areas of the civil rights, women's liberation and sexual liberation movements. By talking about the nation's AIDS hysteria, educators may be able to connect the early response to the epidemic to previous alarmist reactions in American history and the activism that confronted them (California Department of Education, 2015, p. 579).

- To promote civic engagement at this grade level, students can participate in mock trials that recreate some of the landmark cases of the twentieth century detailed in this chapter. They can participate in debates for and against significant governmental policy decisions, such as Prohibition, the creation of the New Deal, efforts to integrate the schools through busing, considerations of racial or gender restrictions on the right to marry, or the question of women, people of color, and lesbian, gay, bisexual, and transgender people serving in the military (California Department of Education, 2015, p. 580).

These excerpts from the eleventh-grade framework illustrate multiple ways in which social studies curriculum can be transformative. Rather than represent topics and individuals as isolated from each other, the curriculum portrays topics and individuals as interconnected and dynamic.

This dynamic view of culture and politics shows how geography, history, economics, and civics are integrated and that different identities of individuals intersect and function to increase or decrease inequitable power relations.

In addition to the guidance on how to make curriculum at different grade levels more inclusive and transformative, the California draft framework provides overarching principles and rationales for the guidelines. The following excerpt is written in the draft framework of Chapter 20, titled "Access and Equity":

Lesbian, Gay, Bisexual, and Transgender Students

All of California's children and adolescents have the fundamental right to be respected and feel safe in their school environment, yet many do not because of their sexual orientation or gender expression. Research indicates that kindergarten through grade six students who are gender nonconforming are less likely than other students to feel very safe at school and more likely to indicate that they sometimes do not want to go to school because they feel unsafe or afraid. Furthermore, they are more likely to be made fun of, called names, or bullied (Gay, Lesbian and Straight Education Network 2012). Lesbian, gay, bisexual, and transgender (LGBT) students between the ages of 13 and 18 also report feeling unsafe and experiencing harassment or assault at school. Like their younger counterparts, they miss days of school to avoid a hostile climate. Notably, students in middle school report higher frequencies of victimization than students in high school (Gay, Lesbian and Straight Education Network 2012).

All California educators have a duty to protect students' right to physical and psychological safety and ensure that each of their students has the opportunity to thrive. The *California Education Code* (EC) Section 200 et seq. prohibits discrimination on the basis of various protected groups, including sexual orientation, gender identity, and gender expression. California recognizes that discrimination and harassment in schools "can have a profound and prolonged adverse effect on students' ability to benefit from public education and maximize their potential" (CDE, 2012). Furthermore, research suggests that victimization based on sexual orientation or gender expression is related to lower academic achievement and educational aspirations as well as poorer psychological well-being (Gay, Lesbian and Straight Education Network 2012). Both teachers and students should understand the terminology used to refer to individuals who are LGBT, and be able to understand the negative effects of slang terms or discriminatory language.

General recommendations from the Gay, Lesbian, and Straight Education Network (Gay, Lesbian and Straight Education Network 2012) for schools regarding students in this heterogeneous population include the following:

- Adopt and implement clear policies and procedures that address bullying and harassment for any reason, thus promoting respectful and safe environments for all students
- Provide professional learning to educators and ensure that all students have access to a welcoming environment and supportive, respectful teachers and staff who will intervene on their behalf
- Increase students' access to an inclusive curriculum (California Senate Bill 48 added language to *Education Code* Section 51204.5 prescribing the inclusion of the contributions of lesbian, gay, bisexual, and transgender Americans to the economic, political, and social development of California and the United States of America, with particular emphasis on portraying the role of these groups in contemporary society)

Additional recommendations include the following:

- Make available and share age-appropriate literature that reflects the diversity of humankind and thoughtfully deals with the complexities and dynamics of intolerance and discrimination
- Teach students by example and through discussion how to treat diverse others

California students who are not themselves in this population may have parents or guardians who are lesbian, gay, bisexual, or transgender. All students and their families need to feel safe, respected, and welcomed in school.

(California Department of Education, 2015, pp. 707–709)

These excerpts from the California draft framework illustrate ways that teachers can create transformative curriculum across social studies disciplines and the rationales for this type of curriculum. They also indicate how intersectionality can be used across the curriculum as a way to increase recognition. As a result of FAIR, the K-12 social science framework is being rewritten to be LGBTQ inclusive. There has also been an increase in access to LGBTQ-inclusive instructional materials and inquiry.

Educator Reflections

I interviewed seven people in California who are educators or policy makers. All agreed to be identified using their real names. Hilary Burge was with the GSA Network and a lead researcher for studies related to LGBTQ-inclusive curriculum. Tarah Fleming and Rick Oculto are teacher educators at Welcoming Schools, a national program that supports LGBTQ-inclusive curriculum in schools. Don Romesburg is an associate professor at Sonoma State University and was co-chair of the Committee on LGBT History, an affiliate of the American Historical Association. He was co-author of recommended revisions for LGBT inclusion in the new social sciences framework. Three educators are from the California Department of Education: Curriculum Frameworks and Instructional Resources Division. Thomas Adams is the division director. Kenneth McDonald is an education programs consultant, and Kristen Cruz Allen is an education administrator.

It is notable that this list of people reflects a much broader range of perspectives than the three teachers that I interviewed in Utah. Whereas this might be seen as a weakness in my representation, I believe that the differences between the lists inherently communicate something about the different contexts of the states. The educators who were willing to talk about LGBTQ-inclusive curriculum in Utah did not want to be named, and their work toward better inclusion was not publicized. The work of the educators who I interviewed in California was very public and represented multiple roles ranging from teacher educators, to historians, to state officials. In what follows, I identified four themes, in addition to the cases I already discussed, that illustrate the context of California. The themes are community contexts, curriculum integration, critical thinking, and recognition through intersectionality.

Community Contexts

Although it is tempting to create a utopia vs. dystopia dichotomy between the two states, the people who I interviewed in both states pointed to a more complex picture of LGBTQ-inclusive curriculum. Communities within states vary in their beliefs about LGBTQ individuals and issues. For example, as a queer male in Utah, I experience great differences between the rural community where I live and the more progressive community of Salt Lake City where I have lived. At one time, I was the only out male faculty member on our campus of over 1,000 faculty. This lack of visibility of LGBTQ faculty on campus and within the community fueled my sense of isolation. These regional differences within states are common, and as the California educators discussed, this is true with California. Hilary remarked:

> There is a perception I think across the country that California is incredibly liberal and forward thinking and moving and doing these innovative things, and that's true, and that's not true in certain places like the Central valley, which probably look very similar [to] places like Utah . . . I think people in other states say, Oh! You can pass laws like that in California because you guys are Californians. I'm thinking, no, go to the rurals, like Central valley areas, and those folks are still very much struggling, and even with this law don't feel that they can implement it . . . California is a very big state with a very different landscape and very urban, very rural, there are so many different pieces of California and different cultures and climates, and there are challenges even with something like the FAIR Education Act existing where people are like, "No, I'm not doing that."

The perception that all of California is progressive denies the discrimination and exclusion that occur in communities where LGBTQ individuals and issues are not welcome, unrecognized, or silenced. As Hilary observes, even a change in the California curriculum framework might not help those who are resistant to the new law. Tarah's comments also indicated a complex picture of the different experiences of teachers:

> When I went down to [ ] to talk to [teachers] they weren't trying to hear about lesson plans for the classroom, they were getting harassed in their own teacher rooms. They were trying to get protected just to go to work, and I felt like this is really not okay that I'm here saying [that] you need to do lessons about gay folks in the classroom when they didn't even feel safe. So, there's like these levels to the bigger picture that I'm hoping that we can be inclusive of all the different experiences.

This indicates the complexity involved with various spheres of inclusion and exclusion. Even if a larger community supports inclusivity in curriculum, this does not mean that LGBTQ students, teachers, and families feel safe, supported, or included within their communities. LGBTQ inclusion is supported by all of the educators who I interviewed, but the expanded awareness that Tarah mentions is necessary if students, teachers, and families are to be recognized, safe, and supported.

Across the differences between and among communities, the FAIR Act provides grounds for educators and students to implement LGBTQ-inclusive curriculum. The following is based upon my conversation with curriculum experts from the California Department of Education. Given the differences across and within communities related to LGBTQ inclusion, they point to ways that the law can support students and educators. Kristen pointed to ways to discuss the changes with those who are resistant. She said, "I think they can always point back to the law and the FAQs. [They] can always give them the FAQs. So, if a parent approached them and said, 'I'm not really pleased about this,' they can go back to the law and the requirements of the law." Kenneth described public reactions to the bill:

> I've gotten a lot of calls on this particular bill and I would say the calls from some parents tended to slant negative while the calls from the teachers and administrators tend to be not even positive but more supportive and/or questioning how they can do it. And that's why we're glad we're able to move forward in the framework because the framework's purpose is to provide guidance to teachers and administrators . . . So, I think that people who are in the education community support the goals of the legislation in a broad sense. Of course, there's going to be opposition and favor, but they're doing it.

Whereas some individuals and communities within the state are resistant to inclusive policies, other communities have embraced the new policy. Thomas discussed his impression of the positive support from the school district where he lives:

> I would say the other thing is that for most people, it tends to be talked about in terms of school climate, not actually curriculum. But in my sampling of my home district, which is the Davis School District, it was very receptive and you know if anything it created increased comfort level especially of people coming from non-traditional families and teachers addressing that in a manner that they felt they could do so forthrightly.

Educators from both states frequently mentioned this responsiveness to students and nontraditional families. The recognition of a diversity of families provides an environment where students can feel safe and respected. Thomas continued:

> I would say the other thing is that the key in all these is that schools are a lot more sensitive on these issues and make sure that their

students are safe. It just seems to become more and more that the law gave a lot of backing. Even though the protection existed beforehand, the curriculum aspect of it seemed to give teachers a lot of confidence about standing up for their students . . . I mean to me, it's one of the best things I've done.

Although different communities in California might react differently to the FAIR Act and implementation of a more LGBTQ-inclusive curriculum, the law provides grounds and supports for students, educators, and districts to create safe and inclusive schools. Some communities might be resistant to these policies, but the context of California is different from that of Utah in that the state provides a rationale and guidance for recognition of LGBTQ individuals and issues.

Curriculum Integration

Educators conceived of inclusive curriculum as being integrated throughout subject areas and the year. As indicated by Utah educators, the themes of inclusion should be woven throughout the curriculum in order for the curriculum to be transformative. This moves away from the dilemmas posed by an additive approach toward inclusion. Tarah referred to the FAIR Act as an opportunity for aligning different strands of inclusion across the curriculum:

> We saw this very amazing opportunity to shift and change what was going on in schools through some of these policies, through some of these materials, and through the genius of the teacher who is able to take children's lit and apply lesson plans. And it's kind of a coming together of multiple pieces, which I think is one of the stories that really needs to be told about how we support teachers to pull the pieces together that are often thrown at them and how they can create braids of alignment of all of the different opportunities whether it'd be common core or math or social sciences. All of these things can come together if we were to support them by saying, "Look, this is how the braid works."

By integrating or braiding inclusion across subject areas, teachers are able to connect multiple subject areas with themes that create a cohesive and inclusive curriculum. As illustrated by the draft of the framework in the previous section, there are multiple opportunities to integrate social studies areas such as civics, geography, economics, and history with subject areas such as language arts and math. In addition to this integration across subject areas, themes of inclusion can run through the entire curriculum. Rick commented upon the need to have the theme of inclusion run throughout the year:

> It's definitely something that we want to emphasize that it's not a matter of history contained within the month, right? It's not Black history month, it's not LGBTQ history month; it has to be curriculum that has to happen throughout the year. It has to be of value within the school, within our communities. That has to be really put out there. And we have some really concrete examples of how creating that braid has really helped communities and the students within those communities really get how important it is to respect one another and how much they can achieve when they do that.

Many of the educators who I interviewed emphasized the goal of intentionally designing curriculum to be integrated across subject areas and time in order to increase student understanding of themselves and their communities. Hilary remarked:

> So it's not just this group that's just siloed and has some kind of very specific identity, but that there's women, there's men, and there's trans people in all of those movements. So when we think about teaching LGBTQ-inclusive curriculum, then it becomes not something you do on a Friday in June or whenever we decide the month is to celebrate LGBTQ people, but that it's part of the way that you tell the story of American history. So when you're talking about the Civil Rights Movement, which everyone does in the 11th grade, you would then talk about Bayard Rustin, and you're talking specifically about the Civil Rights Movement and the march on Washington, which we all learn about and we learn about the famous speech, "I have a dream." And we understand what kind of an organizing brilliance it took for Bayard Rustin to get that many people there and to create that moment, and then also talking about simultaneously what's going on behind the scenes. There's where you sort of fold it in as though it's part of a much larger story and complexifies the way that we understand American history.

As the educators in this section emphasize, LGBTQ inclusion must happen across the curriculum and school year. This leads to a deeper and transformative understanding of social studies and other content areas. Hilary's description of folding and connecting to a larger story creates the kind of critical thinking skills indicated by the new generation of curriculum standards. This leads to the next finding involving social justice and critical thinking.

Critical Thinking

The term critical thinking within the context of curriculum can have two meanings: One meaning is thinking that requires individuals to "acquire such intellectual resources as background knowledge, operational knowledge of appropriate standards, knowledge of key concepts, possession of effective heuristics, and of certain vital habits of mind" (Bailin, Case, Coombs, & Daniels, 1999, p. 285). Another meaning is thinking that involves an analysis of inequitable power relations. Educators communicated both of these meanings when describing LGBTQ-inclusive curriculum.

One of the downsides of an additive compared with a transformative approach to curriculum design and implementation is that additive approaches oversimplify how we understand social studies. It also undermines the range of perspectives in social studies curriculum (Banks, 2004; Camicia, 2007, 2009). The new generation of content standards emphasizes the necessity of students to understand subjects such as history and geography through multiple perspectives. This requires students to think more critically about knowledge. Rather than consume the knowledge that social scientists produce, students learn how to do the work of social scientists. Don discussed this as follows:

> We definitely looked at C3 and putting together our introduction and checking it against the way that we put the framework revisions together. This works really well actually with the C3. It is important that history education moves away from just thinking of Black people and women and gay people and immigrants and instead shifts to thinking of questions of how gender, sexuality, nation, race are interlocking analytical categories through which meaning, belonging and marginalization are produced through the nation state or communities. The more it can do those things, the more it's really doing what C3 seeks. I feel like it is looking for that kind of flexible critical analytic thinking that requires contextualization and analysis of primary documents. It challenges certain ways of learning about the past that you are being taught and unpacking those things and collaborating to explore those things.

The ability to connect multiple lenses relates well with the previous section where educators talked about integration. By integrating or braiding inclusive and critical lenses throughout the curriculum, the curriculum becomes more equitable while increasing student critical thinking skills. Hilary referred to the work that Don and his committee did in proposing changes to the social science framework. She said, "I think that one of the things that they did so well in here was really talk about, like I mentioned, incorporating LGBTQ-inclusive curriculum as a much larger sort of story and then also having a racial and economic justice lens and talking about a gender lens." The larger story involves using lenses that illustrate social inequalities related to race, class, gender identities, sexual identities, ability, language, and geopolitical belonging.

Recognition Through Intersectionality

The themes that have emerged so far support a move in curriculum toward recognition through intersectionality. Rather than designing curriculum to include identities and school subjects in silos, they need to be integrated through the lens of intersectionality. Most of the educators who I interviewed in Utah and California described the need to recognize people and groups as situated within complex and inequitable geographies and histories. Hilary describes the movement toward intersectionality in inclusive curriculum:

> I wanted to work at GSA Network because we had made it a priority to do racial and economic justice work. I think that there are [a] lot of queer organizations that really, including us because we have room to grow as well, but there are lot of queer organizations who need to grow. I think a lot in their work that they do in racial and economic justice and understanding that queer people are also people of color. I also in some of the recent research I have been doing have been really partnering a lot with racial and economic justice organizations who desperately also want to develop their queer analysis. So seeing those two movements as really having a lot more in common but having maybe some areas of need in growth where we can both teach each other and then thinking about the intersectionality of race, class, and gender. Specifically in this report that we wrote, and the research we did on the FAIR Education Act, one of the chapters in the section is on the concept of culturally relevant curriculum.

The need for intersectionality as a strand running across the curriculum is closely tied to recognition and social justice. Social studies curriculum provides an optimal place for students to examine the ways that multiple perspectives and lenses provide a deeper understanding of social inequalities. Don gives an example of how these lenses increase our understanding of how historical phenomena are intertwined:

> One of the things that bringing LGBT people into history curriculum necessarily does is it requires you to think about sexuality as a field of social power. That means that you don't just put in heroes and icons, right? You have to understand, for example, how anti-cross dressing laws formed in states around the US West in the second half of the 19th century relates to anxieties around women in their mobility, relates to anxieties about immigration, and anxieties about gender diversity and sexual transgression.

Rather than an additive approach, Don illustrates how history curriculum can use a transformative lens that recognizes power relations. Student examination of networks of power relations can increase student understanding of social inequalities. The intersections of these different networks provide a complex picture of individuals and communities.

Conclusion

The cases that I presented at the beginning of this chapter are not meant to create a utopia (California) verses a dystopia (Utah) related to the cultural and political contexts in which LGBTQ-inclusive curriculum is or isn't taught. As indicated in this chapter, there are many differences between and within communities that lead to inclusion and exclusion. The socially constructed hierarchies that institutionalize racism, sexism, classism, heteronormativity, cisgenderism, ableism, and nationalism are dominant across society. Many of the California educators who I interviewed indicated the complex regional differences within the state. Whereas many policies in California are progressive compared with other states, according to participants, many communities stand in the way of LGBTQ inclusion inside and outside of schools. This is an illustration of the complex relationship between educational policy and implementation. Whereas teachers promoting LGBTQ-inclusive curriculum point to inclusive laws as an important way to defend themselves against stakeholders who are opposed to these laws, the laws do not always get implemented in classrooms where teachers and communities are not inclined to support inclusion.

The educators in this chapter indicate ways to design curriculum that is integrated, encourages critical thinking, and focuses upon intersectionality. These goals are aligned with a new generation of standards that emphasize multiple perspectives and inquiry. By using the lens of power relations during inquiry involving multiple perspectives, the social studies curriculum can increase recognition and student understandings of social justice. In the next chapter, I provide curriculum recommendations that use this concept as a guiding principle for curriculum design and implementation.

References

Adams, T. E. (2013). Frames of homosexuality-comparing *Los Angeles Times'* coverage of California's proposition 6 (1978) and proposition 8 (2008). *Sexuality & Culture, 17*(2), 213–228.

Bailin, S., Case, R., Coombs, J., & Daniels, L. B. (1999). Conceptualizing critical thinking. *Journal of Curriculum Studies, 31*(3), 285–302.

Banks, J. A. (2004). *Approaches to multicultural education reform multicultural education: Issues and perspectives* (5th ed., pp. 225–246). Hoboken, NJ: John Wiley & Sons, Inc.

Biegel, S. (2010). *The right to be out: Sexual orientation and gender identity in America's public schools.* Minneapolis, MN: University of Minnesota Press.

Burdge, H., Sinclair, K., Laub, C., & Russell, S. T. (2012). *Lessons that matter: LGBTQ inclusivity and school safety.* San Francisco, CA: Gay-Straight Alliance Network and California Safe Schools Coalition Report No. 14.

California Department of Education. (2011). Frequently asked questions: Senate Bill 48. Retrieved from http://www.cde.ca.gov/ci/cr/cf/senatebill48faq.asp

California Department of Education. (2015). 2014–2016 History-social sciences framework second field review draft approved by the Instructional Quality Commission November 20, 2015. Retrieved from California Department of Education http://www.cde.ca.gov/ci/hs/cf/hssfw2ndreview.asp

Camicia, S. P. (2007). Deliberating immigration policy: Locating instructional materials within global and multicultural perspectives. *Theory and Research in Social Education, 35*(1), 96–111.

Camicia, S. P. (2009). Identifying soft democratic education: Uncovering the range of civic and cultural choices in instructional materials. *The Social Studies, 100*(3), 136–142.

Cianciotto, J., & Cahill, S. (2012). *LGBT youth in America's schools.* Ann Arbor, MI: The University of Michigan Press.

Eaklor, V. L. (2008). *Queer America: A people's GLBT hisory of the United States.* New York: The New Press.

Gay, Lesbian and Straight Education Network. (2012). *Playgrounds and prejudice: Elementary school climate in the United States,* New York, NY: Author.

GSA Network. (2015a). Creating inclusive GSA's: The basics. Retrieved from https://http://www.gsanetwork.org/resources/creating-inclusive-gsas/creating-inclusive-gsas-basics

GSA Network. (2015b). History and accomplishments. Retrieved from https://http://www.gsanetwork.org/about-us/history

GSA Network. (2015c). A history of California legislation related to LGBTQ youth. Retrieved from http://gsanetwork.org/files/getinvolved/Legislative History Guide for CA LGBTQ youth legislation.pdf

Hirshman, L. (2012). *Victory: The triumphant gay revolution.* New York: Harper-Collins Publishers.

Kosciw, J. G., Greytak, E. A., Palmer, N. A., & Boesen, M. J. (2014). *The 2013 national school climate survey: The experiences of lesbian, gay, bisexual and transgender youth in our nation's schools.* New York: GLSEN (Gay, Lesbian & Straight Education Network).

Kull, R. M., Kosciw, J. G., & Greytak, E. A. (2015). *From statehouse to schoolhouse: Anti-bullying policy efforts in the U.S. states and school districts.* New York: GLSEN (Gay, Lesbian & Straight Education Network).

Miceli, M. (2005). *Standing out, standing together: The social and political impact of Gay-Straight Alliances.* New York: Routledge.

Pupil Rights: Sex-Segregated School Programs and Activities, AB 1266 (California Legislative Information 2013).

School Employees—Homosexuality California Initiative 160. (1977). UC hastings scholarship repository. Retrieved from http://repository.uchastings.edu/cgi/viewcontent.cgi?article=1350&context=ca_ballot_inits

Snow, D. A. (2004). Framing processes, ideology, and discursive fields. In D. A. Snow, S. A. Soule & H. Kriesi (Eds.), *The Blackwell companion to social movements* (pp. 380–412). Malden, MA: Blackwell.

Tarrow, S. G. (1998). *Power in movement: Social movements and contentious politics* (2nd ed.). New York: Cambridge University Press.

Tilly, C. (2004). *Social movements, 1768–2004.* Boulder, CO: Paradigm Publishers.

Uribe, V., & Harbeck, K. M. (1992). Addressing the needs of lesbian, gay, and bisexual youth: The origins of project 10 and school-based intervention. In K. M. Harbeck (Ed.), *Coming out of the classroom closet: Gay and lesbian students, teachers, and curricula.* Bringhampton, NY: Harrington Park Press.

5   Social Justice and LGBTQ Issues in Schools

The classroom, with all its limitations, remains a location of possibility. In that field of possibility we have the opportunity to labor for freedom, to demand of ourselves and our comrades, an openness of mind and heart that allows us to face reality even as we collectively imagine ways to move beyond boundaries, to transgress. This is education as the practice of freedom.

bell hooks (1994, p. 207)

The illustrations from Utah and California point to disparities in the degree of recognition within different cultural and political contexts. Educators and students are embedded in different contexts that either hinder or help them move beyond the boundaries that maintain inequitable power relations in curriculum and society. In this chapter, I conclude by examining the impact of exclusionary and inclusionary curricula upon students. I then address the following questions from Chapter 1: How does inclusive curriculum affect students in different cultural and political contexts? How do public policies around schools respond to shifts toward greater LGBTQ recognition? What does school resistance to these shifts tell us about the legitimacy of public education? How can we facilitate schools and curriculum that support inclusion, recognition, and social justice?

The Impact of Misrecognition and Recognition on Students

How does inclusive curriculum affect students in different cultural and political contexts? There is little doubt that LGBTQ students experience exclusion from school communities through a lack of representation or misrepresentation in the curriculum. Illustrations in the proceeding chapters point to this. The Gay, Lesbian and Straight Education Network (GLSEN) (Kosciw, Greytak, Palmer, & Boesen, 2014) conducted a national survey in 2013 of 7,898 youth between the ages of 13 and 21. The following findings indicate areas of concern related to LGBTQ student health and academic performance:

School Safety

- 55.5% of LGBT students felt unsafe at school because of their sexual orientation, and 37.8% because of their gender expression.
- 30.3% of LGBT students missed at least one entire day of school in the past month because they felt unsafe or uncomfortable, and over a tenth (10.6%) missed four or more days in the past month.
- Over a third avoided gender-segregated spaces in school because they felt unsafe or uncomfortable (bathrooms: 35.4%, locker rooms: 35.3%).
- Most reported avoiding school functions and extracurricular activities (68.1% and 61.2%, respectively) because they felt unsafe or uncomfortable (p. xvi).

When schools are left to mirror the sources of discrimination within society, they can be dangerous places for LGBTQ students. If schools don't consciously foster a climate of safety and recognition, LGBTQ students face mental and physical harm. Unfortunately, the hidden curriculum found in many school policies perpetuates climates of discrimination, fear, and a lack of LGBTQ recognition. GLSEN (Kosciw et al., 2014, pp. xvii–xviii) findings indicate this:

Discriminatory School Policies and Practices

- 55.5% of LGBT students reported personally experiencing any LGBT-related discriminatory policies or practices at school (see below), and almost two thirds (65.2%) said other students had experienced these policies and practices at school.
- 28.2% of students reported being disciplined for public displays of affection that were not disciplined among non-LGBT students.
- 18.1% of students were prevented from attending a dance or function with someone of the same gender.
- 17.8% of students were restricted from forming or promoting a GSA.
- 17.5% of students were prohibited from discussing or writing about LGBT topics in school assignments.

- 15.5% of students were prevented from wearing clothing or items supporting LGBT issues 9.2% of students reported being disciplined for simply identifying as LGBT.
- Some policies particularly targeted transgender students:
    - 42.2% of transgender students had been prevented from using their preferred name (10.8% of LGBT students overall);
    - 59.2% of transgender students had been required to use a bathroom or locker room of their legal sex (18.7% of students overall); and
    - 31.6% of transgender students had been prevented from wearing clothes considered inappropriate based on their legal sex (19.2% of students overall).

Although public schools are charged with the health, safety, and learning of all students, some schools continue discriminatory practices that harm LGBTQ youth. These practices are also prevalent in schools when curriculum excludes LGBTQ perspectives and issues. The following GLSEN (Kosciw et al., 2014, pp. xix–xx) findings indicate the influences of exclusion and inclusion of LGBTQ individuals and issues within the curriculum:

Inclusive Curricular Resources

Availability

- Only 18.5% of LGBT students were taught positive representations about LGBT people, history, or events in their schools; 14.8% had been taught negative content about LGBT topics.
- Less than half (44.2%) of students reported that they could find information about LGBT-related issues in their school library.
- Less than half of students (45.3%) with Internet access at school reported being able to access LGBT related information online via school computers.

Utility

- LGBT students in schools with an LGBT-inclusive curriculum:
    - Were less likely to hear "gay" used in a negative way often or frequently (54.7% compared to 78.5% of other students);
    - Were less likely to hear homophobic remarks such as "fag" or "dyke" often or frequently (46.3% vs. 68.7%);

- Were less likely to hear negative remarks about gender expression often or frequently (43.5% vs. 59.2%);
- Were less likely to feel unsafe because of their sexual orientation (34.8% vs. 59.8%);
- Were less likely to miss school in the past month (16.7% of students with an inclusive curriculum missed school in past month because they felt unsafe or uncomfortable compared to 32.9% of other students);
- Were more likely to report that their classmates were somewhat or very accepting of LGBT people (75.2% vs. 39.6%); and
- Felt more connected to their school community.

- LGBT high school seniors were more likely to be interested in studying STEM (Science, Technology, Engineering, or Math) or Social Science in college if their relevant high school classes had included positive LGBT content (35.8% vs. 18.5% for STEM majors; 29.0 vs. 19.7% for Social Science majors).

These findings are similar to those of other studies (Burdge, Sinclair, Laub, & Russell, 2012; Cianciotto & Cahill, 2012; Mayo, 2014; Williams, Connolly, Pepler, & Craig, 2005). When the formal and informal curricula of schools do not recognize LGBTQ individuals and perspectives, discrimination mirrors dominant cultural and political contexts within society. Conversely, when LGBTQ individuals and issues are recognized in the curriculum, student safety, health, and learning improve.

Recognition and School Legitimacy in Utah and California

Curriculum represents a worldview about what is important for students to learn. Different worldviews can lead to different ideas about what the curriculum should and shouldn't contain. This necessarily leads to difficult conversations in curriculum that reflect difficult conversations within society. The ideas, learning activities, and content that are left out of the curriculum express as much of a worldview as what is left in the curriculum (Eisner, 2002). When LGBTQ individuals and issues are left out of the curriculum, students and educators are given the message that these individuals and issues are unimportant, or worse, abnormal. The norms then function to dehumanize LGBTQ individuals. The illustrations from Utah and California provide an opportunity to see how inclusion and exclusion are reflected in the official and unofficial curricula in different communities. The official and unofficial curricula of Utah and California reflect different political and cultural contexts. The GLSEN findings noted earlier (Kosciw et al., 2014) emphasize the importance of inclusive schooling in the improved health, safety, and learning of students.

My examination was limited by the illustrations from the examples that I provided, but this examination is meant to open conversations concerning how the illustrations of inclusion and exclusion might transfer to other cultural and political contexts. The purpose was not to create a utopian vs. dystopian binary between states. In both cases, accounts of inclusiveness varied within each state. The illustrations from the different states have implications for policy, social studies curriculum, democratic education, and social justice because differences in context profoundly affect the lives of LGBTQ students and educators.

Examples from Utah illustrate that although there are pockets of LGBTQ inclusion in Salt Lake City, the educational policies and struggles around LGBTQ issues constrain the curriculum in ways that exclude LGBTQ students, educators, and community members. Although pockets of resistance emerge, such as the GSA victory at East High, the dominant culture within Utah constrains such victories. These victories are also embedded in a dominant cultural and political context that demands the exclusion and lack of recognition of LGBTQ individuals.

The exclusionary beliefs and practices that dominate culture and politics in Utah are perhaps best reflected in an LDS church declaration in fall of 2015. The declaration states that children living in homes with parents in a same-sex relationship are barred "from being baptized, confirmed, ordained to the church's all-male priesthood or recommended for missionary service without the permission of the faith's highest leaders—the governing First Presidency" (Dobner, 2015, paragraph 15). This policy is particularly disappointing because children bear the brunt of discrimination against their parents who are in same-sex relationships. In addition, the policy brands people in same-sex relationships as apostates. These forms of discrimination and exclusion form the backdrop for public schools and curriculum. It is no wonder that educators are fearful of LGBTQ inclusion in such an environment. The official and unofficial curricula are exclusionary in Utah. The message to students and educators is clear. LGBTQ individuals and issues are not valued, and worse, they are pathologized.

My findings from different state contexts raise important questions about the legitimacy of public education systems that perpetuate exclusion and inequality. Legitimacy within a democracy is closely tied to the degree to which those who are governed are recognized in school policies and curriculum. An underlying assumption of democracy and democratic education is that those influenced by governance structures have a voice in that governance (Camicia, 2009). Another assumption is that curriculum functions as a system of governance in that it regulates what knowledge is deemed valuable and what knowledge is not (Apple, 1979). When voices and perspectives are excluded from curriculum, critical democratic education suffers.

Although there has been an increase in inclusive laws that protect LGBTQ individuals, these laws are not reflected in Utah schools. One of the most glaring examples of this is the national law protecting marriage equality. Within the context of this law, how is it that Utah schools can claim legitimacy when same-sex relationships are barred from curriculum? What rationale could possibly be provided that would make such exclusions anything other than a reflection of a discriminatory cultural and political context? Although these discriminatory practices are often framed as religious freedom, the end result is discrimination that harms students in public schools. At this level, the civil and human rights of students are violated by schools that are charged with student health, safety, and learning.

In contrast, the official curriculum of California contains multiple indicators that foster inclusion of LGBTQ individuals and issues. The framework and laws prohibiting discrimination provide teachers with the tools and rationales that they need to increase the inclusiveness of their curriculum. It does not mean that every community within California will accept or teach under these standards and laws, but educators in communities that don't welcome recognition are given the legal backing to increase recognition in their curriculum. The responsiveness of the California Department of Education toward LGBTQ inclusion marks an increase in legitimacy of its democratic governance. The recognition of those governed is reflected in state standards. In addition to the official curriculum in the form of standards, California has a long history of reform toward inclusion. It is within this political and cultural context in which the official and unofficial curriculum is embedded.

In the case of California, educational policies are leaning toward more inclusion, which provides some opportunities for inclusion and removes some of the constraints. In Utah, educational policies lean toward LGBT exclusion, which provides few opportunities for inclusion and many constraints. The Briggs Initiative provides an illustration of the different timelines between the two states. As discussed in Chapter 4, in 1978, California voters voted down the Briggs Initiative, which sought to exclude lesbian and gay teachers. In contrast, Utah currently prohibits inclusion. This is illustrated in the law saying that the curriculum must not "promote homosexuality." When these exclusions are intertwined with the myriad other exclusions related to social injustices such as race, class, gender, ability, language, and geopolitical belonging, oppression in schools is intensified.

Utah and California illustrate complex webs of power and inequality as they relate to what students learn in schools. This relationship between power/knowledge is apparent as the "norms" of different communities are reflected in the curriculum. Although on the surface the curriculum appears neutral, it is far from neutral because it functions to maintain social inequalities (Apple, 2004). In order to uncover these inequalities, schools need curriculum that recognizes the uniqueness of every student and their positionality rather than privilege one identity and positionality as a norm in which all are measured. When schools operate under an ethics of recognition, they provide learning environments that can be described as third spaces where multiple identities, positionalities, and ways of knowing are in dialogue. Fine, Weis, Centrie, and Roberts (2000) illustrate this third space as an:

> interrogation into the *borders* of the space, trying to discern what defines, marks, separates and joins this space to surrounding structures and social formations; investigation into the *interior relations* within the space, relations of hierarchy, justice, reciprocity, trust, and conflict; analyses of *individual and group identity* construction, deconstruction, and reconstruction for youth and adults within the space; and research into the *activist joints* of this space with other such spaces, counter-hegemonic ideologies, and social movements.
>
> (p. 133, emphasis in the original)

Queer theory provides a lens for understanding how these critical democratic third spaces might be achieved through student examinations of the norms that lead to a lack of recognition. LGBTQ students are disproportionately affected by norms that enforce dominant notions of gender and sexuality. They are often isolated and lack relationships with people who identify with genders and/or sexualities that do not reflect the dominant norms. Discourse analysis and third spaces could offer support for the dialogue that will alleviate isolation and work toward social justice. All students benefit from this dialogue as they participate in critically democratic education. Students who identify with dominant gender and sexuality norms benefit from an increase of perspectives in the curriculum. As a result, critical democracy has a place to develop in the classroom. LGBTQ students benefit from schools that recognize them and support an increase in student health, safety, and learning.

Increasing LGBTQ Recognition

The educators I interviewed provided important insights into how to increase recognition and social justice in the public school curriculum. I synthesize these insights with the concepts in Chapter 2, which focus on critical democratic education and queer theory. Young (2000) provides a useful framework for understanding how to synthesize these concepts and recommendations related to increased inclusion and recognition. This framework involves an examination of curriculum through the lenses of external and internal exclusion in order to foster inclusion. I conclude by applying Young's process of greeting, rhetoric, and narrative as a way to create a critical democratic education.

The illustrations from Utah and California provide multiple examples of external and internal exclusion. In Utah, educators have interpreted the banning of curriculum that "promotes homosexuality" as a prohibition on the inclusion of any LGBTQ issues. This ban is an example of external exclusion because the voices of LGBTQ individuals are not allowed in the curriculum. Although this ban did not extend to school libraries, the conclusion of the book-banning conflict ended with inclusion in libraries but exclusion in classrooms. In the case of California, curriculum standards attempt to address external exclusion in curriculum by including LGBTQ history in the standards.

Internal exclusion involves exclusion on the level of norms and discourse. Young (2000) describes a process of exclusion where "the terms of discourse make assumptions some do not share, the interaction privileges specific styles of expression, the participation of some people is dismissed as out of order" (p. 53). The illustrations from Utah indicate a culture of fear where homophobic discourses overpower discourses of recognition. This renders discourses of recognition as abnormal or unintelligible. My positionality as a White, queer male creates a fluctuating and relational experience with inclusion and exclusion. Although as a White male I experience an unearned degree of recognition, I also experience a lack of recognition as queer. As an associate professor at a university in Utah, the pressure for me to self-sensor is powerful in the presence of students and colleagues. My comments aimed at inequitable norms and power relations within public schools are often met with discourses of community values, standards, or efficiency. These discourses function to make my comments "out of order" or "theoretical." People who reflect dominant identities and benefit from inequitable power relations judge them this way. My queer perspectives are "theoretical" to such people because my observations are from a perspective that reflects my queerness. They are not "real" but "theoretical" to the dominant culture. I provide this as a personal example of internal exclusion. Related to the overall theme of this book, the internal exclusion that I experience is relational, contextual, and dependent upon my positionality (Camicia, 2014a, 2014b).

A way to reduce external and internal exclusion is to create a transformational curriculum that focuses upon the ways that the power/knowledge relationship and norms perpetuate social inequalities. Young (2000) provides guidance upon how to accomplish this, and her process is well aligned with the ethics of recognition that I discuss in Chapter 2. The first aspect involves *greeting*. In this process, people acknowledge an ethical relationship to recognize each other. She writes, "A speaker announces her presence as ready to listen and take responsibility for her relationship to her interlocutors, at the same time that it announces her distance from the others, their irreducible particularity" (p. 59). This reflects an ethics of recognition with a queer lens. Although we have an ethical responsibility in communication to recognize another, we must understand that this recognition is never complete and always changing.

As applied to LGBTQ inclusivity in classrooms, *greeting* emphasizes the need for students and teachers to commit to an ethical obligation of teaching and learning within a complex process of recognition. The educators in Chapters 3 and 4 emphasized the need for students to examine intersectionality and positionality. The unique experiences and identities of students and educators are embedded in a complex web of power relations. When students and educators are able to examine these realities within the areas of history, geography, economics, and civics, they increase their chances of transgressing the boundaries that perpetuate social injustices. Curriculum usually ignores these realities by portraying knowledge as 'neutral,' although as the illustrations from Utah and California indicate, the curriculum is never neutral but rather the reflection of cultural and political contexts. By committing to recognition, students and educators can embrace the complexity of the world rather than pretend that this complexity doesn't exist.

A second aspect of Young's (2000) process involves *rhetoric*. This focuses upon opportunities and constraints involved with norms of communication. She writes, "One reason to bring the category of rhetoric explicitly into focus is to notice in a situation of political conflict how some people can be excluded from the public by dismissal of their style" (p. 70). As was apparent in the illustrations from Utah, dominant discourses constrain what can and cannot be said. These constraints place a considerable roadblock to recognition because the expression of nondominant discourses is prohibited and deemed to be deficient, abnormal, or inefficient.

In order to increase recognition in public schools, curriculum can foster student and teacher exploration into the ways that discourses marginalize people and perpetuate inequitable power relations. In a past study, I discuss how educators can teach students discourse analysis as a way to uncover inequitable power relations (Camicia & Zhu, 2012). When students are provided a third space where they can examine the relationships between power/knowledge and discourse, they can start to deconstruct norms that perpetuate social inequalities. This examination can create a third space where each student's unique knowledge, experiences, perspectives, intersectionality, and positionality are valued and used as a source for greater recognition.

The educators from Utah and California indicated multiple ways that attention to discourse can increase inclusion. This is also evident in the revised California framework. In their report recommending revisions to the framework, Romesburg, Rupp, and Donahue (2014) write:

> A proper retelling of history also requires a transformational approach that incorporates what scholars of the past now understand about the profound influence and change over time of sexuality as a field of social power and meaning making (related to gender, race, and other aspects of difference). LGBT history is central to this. Students can only truly understand families, communities, social practices, and politics, for example, by understanding how they shaped and were shaped by same-sex relations and gender diversity—and how this changed over time.
>
> (p. 6)

By examining the ways that power relations have included the meaning making of historical and contemporary individuals and communities, students gain a better understanding of social studies and critical democratic education. The structures that traditional social studies curriculum masks with grand narratives, additive approaches, and claims to neutrality are given a third space where students learn to think critically as social scientists. Rather than be passive recipients of subjects such as history, economics, civics, and geography, students can develop the skills of historians, economists, citizens, and geographers.

Discourses of 'normality,' 'objectivity,' 'efficiency,' and 'standardization' have served as tools in curriculum and school policy to construct and reinforce other discourses that perpetuate inequality and oppression. Although on the surface, they feign neutrality, these discourses function to perpetuate underlying discourses of racism, classism, ableism, sexism, cisgenderism, heterosexism, nationalism, and ethnocentrism in curriculum. People who are marginalized by these discourses can disrupt them by creating counternarratives that challenge oppressive narratives. The discourses that emerge from these counternarratives function to blur the boundaries of oppression that have appeared as neutral in curriculum and school policies. The third aspect of Young's (2000) model involves *narrative*. She writes, "Storytelling is often an important bridge in such cases between the mute experience of being wronged and political arguments about justice" (p. 72). Rather than portraying discourses and narratives in the curriculum as neutral, the privileging of nondominant narratives and discourses shows students and educators that curriculum and school policies are political statements. These political statements are a reflection of inequitable power relations.

Bhabha (2003) places narrative as a human right and a way to address inequalities in education and society. The right for individuals to tell their narratives is tied to a larger project of human rights and the strengthening of democracy within communities. He writes:

> To protect the 'right to narrate' is to protect a range of democratic imperatives: it assumes that there is an equitable access to those institutions—schools, universities, museums, libraries, theatres— that give you a sense of a collective history and the means to turn those materials into a narrative of your own. Such an assured, empowered sense of 'selfhood', the knowledge that to tell your story is to know that there is a 'public culture' in which it will be heard and could be acted upon, depends upon the nation's guardianship of what Article 5 of the International Convention on Economic, Social and Political Rights defines as 'the right to take part in cultural life'.
> (pp. 180–181)

Bhabha's (2003) "right to narrate" reflects an ethic of recognition that supports third spaces in educational and community settings. Narratives help challenge the dehumanizing discourses that portray a 'norm' that positions those not in the norm as 'abnormal' and less than human.

Critical democratic and queer discourses increase the variety of non-dominant discourses by challenging norms and examining the knowledge/power relationships expressed in dominant discourses and binary oppositions. This can be accomplished when analyses of positionalities and discourses are central to the curriculum and school context. Through discourse analysis and dialogue in classrooms, there is an opportunity for recognition. This recognition would involve examining norms, binary relationships, discourses, intersectionalities, and power/

knowledge relationships. For example: *How do norms of discipline in a school disproportionately affect some groups more than others? Are males disciplined more than females? Do transphobic, sexist, and homophobic aggressions go undisciplined?* In another example: *How are groups represented differently in the curriculum? Does the norm of inclusion overrepresent epistemology and history from a White, cisgender, heterosexual, male, middle-class, English speaking, able-bodied perspective? How have the definitions and categories related to gender and sexuality been constructed over time? How have these constructions created exclusionary norms?* An examination of questions such as these within the curriculum can provide an insight into the dominant discourses that perpetuate inequality, as well as related power/knowledge relationships. They are also questions that can be examined through all of the social studies subject areas.

The illustrations of inclusion and recognition from Utah and California show how greeting, rhetoric, and narrative can be strands that run through the curriculum in ways that promote social justice and third spaces. The aspect of greeting is evident in the ways that educators promoted an ethical relationship between students, educators, and the community toward mutual recognition. Rhetoric was evident in the ways that educators encouraged students to challenge normalizing discourses that perpetuate social injustices. Narrative was evident in the ways that dominant narratives are challenged by marginalized narratives of the past and present. The focus upon intersectionality across examples emphasized the importance of counternarrative in curriculum. These strands of curriculum support recognition, blurring of boundaries, opening of third spaces, transformational student learning, and social justice.

The cases of California and Utah indicate how different political and cultural contexts might influence what and how students learn about LGBTQ issues and individuals. The differences between the two states illustrate the inequalities and obstacles in learning environments for LGBTQ students, as well as implications for critical democratic education for all students. Although in different contexts, the educators in both found social studies classrooms to be places where inclusion and exclusion could be examined. They often referred to possibilities for conversations about the intersectionalities of privileges and oppressions. This intersectionality can provide a complex understanding of how discourses of 'normality' are used as tools of oppression that provide 'reasons' for making some humans and their perspectives more valuable than others.

Given that public schools are charged with creating inclusive environments for *all* students, recognition should be privileged over the discriminatory cultural and political preferences of a particular community. On an epistemological level, lack of recognition in schools functions to dehumanize students and educators. Norms function to exclude students from the curriculum by creating dominant cultures and identities as the norm in which the values of students and their perspectives are regarded or disregarded. In order for curriculum to function democratically and inclusively, it must encourage a paradox that seeks for recognition, but also seeks to deconstruct representations.

The hostility that LGBTQ students experience at school sends messages to all students that LGBTQ youth are not valued by the school community, or in other words, they are less than human. This provides the basis for many forms of assault on LGBTQ youth, both physical and mental. This oppression intensifies when the histories or experiences of LGBTQ people are either absent or disparaged in social studies curriculum. Evidence that LGBTQ-inclusive curriculum can ameliorate hostile learning environments for LGBTQ students and increase their academic performance is compelling. Burdge, Sinclair, Laub, Russell, and Moody (2013) found that "LGBTQ-inclusive curriculum was identified by students as one strategy that could substantially improve safety, engagement, learning, academic achievement, self-esteem, and success in school and beyond" (p. 31).

This form of recognition translates to LGBTQ individuals in educational settings when the curriculum recognizes or makes intelligible past and present issues and influences that have affected the lives of LGBTQ individuals. The recognition of LGBTQ individuals is especially important in social studies education because LGBTQ individuals and issues can be acknowledged in subject areas such as geography (Schmidt, 2015), economics (Drucker, 2011), civics (Maguth & Taylor, 2013; Mayo, 2013; Richardson, 2012; Russell, Toomey, Crockett, & Laub, 2010), controversial issues (Hess, 2009), and history (Bailey & Graves, 2012; Donahue, 2014; Romesburg et al., 2014; Schmidt, 2014; Stern, 2009). This is not to say that LGBTQ individuals are absent in these subject areas, but it is to say that they have been included without acknowledgement of their gender or sexual identities. Without this acknowledgement, students are left assuming that the geographies, economics, civics, and histories of LGBTQ individuals match the normative structures defined by patriarchy and heteronormativity. This renders LGBTQ individuals as unrecognizable, which poses a fundamental problem when education is aimed at preparing individuals to participate effectively in democratic communities. Public schools have an ethical obligation to the communities that they serve to promote an ethic of recognition in curriculum and school policies.

References

Apple, M. W. (1979). *Ideology and curriculum*. Boston: Routledge & Kegan Paul.

Apple, M. W. (2004). *Ideology and curriculum* (3rd ed.). New York: Routledge-Falmer.

Bailey, L., & Graves, K. (2012). Introduction: Society can only be as free and open as its schools. In E. R. Meiners & Q. Therese (Eds.), *Sexualities in education: A reader* (pp. 43–45). New York: Peter Lang Publishing, Inc.

Bhabha, H. K. (2003). On writing rights. *Globalizing rights: The Oxford Amnesty lectures 1999* (pp. 162–183). New York: Oxford University Press.

Burdge, H., Sinclair, K., Laub, C., & Russell, S. T. (2012). *Lessons that matter: LGBTQ inclusivity and school safety*. San Francisco, CA: Gay-Straight Alliance Network and California Safe Schools Coaltion Report No. 14.

Burdge, H., Sinclair, K., Laub, C., Russell, S. T., & Moody, R. (2013). *Implementing lessons that matter: The impct of LGBTQ-inclusive curriculum on student safety, well-being, and achievement*. San Francisco, CA: Gay-Straight Alliance Nework and Tucson, AZ: Frances McClelland Institute for Children, Youth, and Families at the University of Arizona.

Camicia, S. P. (2009). Identifying soft democratic education: Uncovering the range of civic and cultural choices in instructional materials. *The Social Studies, 100*(3), 136–142.

Camicia, S. P. (2014a). My pedagogical creed: Positionality, recognition, and dialogue in democratic education. In S. Totten (Ed.), *The importance of teaching social issues: Our pedagogical creeds* (pp. 166–175). New York: Routledge.

Camicia, S. P. (2014b). Navigating/embodying controversy in classrooms in the United States and Philippines: Using autoethnography to understand the complexities of democracy in different contexts. In T. Misco & J. De Groof (Eds.), *Cross-cultural case studies of teaching controversial issues: Pathways and challenges to democratic citizenship education* (pp. 95–109). Oisterwijk, Netherlands: Legal Wolf Publishers.

Camicia, S. P., & Zhu, J. (2012). Synthesizing multicultural, global, and civic perspectives in the elementary school curriculum and educational research. *The Qualitative Report, 17*, 1–19.

Cianciotto, J., & Cahill, S. (2012). *LGBT youth in America's schools*. Ann Arbor, MI: The University of Michigan Press.

Dobner, J. (2015, November 14). New Mormon policy makes apostates of married same-sex couples, bars children from rites. *Salt Lake Tribune*. Retrieved from http://www.sltrib.com/csp/mediapool/sites/sltrib/pages/printfriendly.csp?id=3144035

Donahue, D. M. (2014). Learning from harvey milk: The limits and opportunities of one hero to teach about LGBTQ people and issues. *The Social Studies, 105*(1), 36–44.

Drucker, P. (2011). The fracturing of LGBT identities under neoliberal capitalism. *Historical Materialism, 19*(4), 3–32.

Eisner, E. W. (2002). *The educational imagination: On the design and evaluation of school programs* (3rd ed.). Upper Saddle River, NJ: Prentice Hall.

Fine, M., Weis, L., Centrie, C., & Roberts, R. (2000). Educating beyond the borders of schooling. *Anthropology & Education Quarterly, 31*(2), 131–151.

Hess, D. E. (2009). Teaching about same-sex marriage as policy and constitutional issue. *Social Education, 73*(7), 344–349.

hooks, b. (1994). Teaching to transgress: Education as the practice of freedom. New York: Routledge.

Kosciw, J. G., Greytak, E. A., Palmer, N. A., & Boesen, M. J. (2014). *The 2013 national school climate survey: The experiences of lesbian, gay, bisexual and transgender youth in our nation's schools*. New York: GLSEN (Gay, Lesbian & Straight Education Network).

Maguth, B. M., & Taylor, N. (2013). Bringing LGBTQ topics into the social studies classroom. *The Social Studies, 105*(1), 23–28.

Mayo, C. (2014). *LGBTQ youth and education: Policies and practices*. New York: Teachers Collge Press.

Mayo, J. B. (2013). Critical pedagogy enacted in the gay-straight alliance-new possibilities for a third space in teacher development. *Educational Researcher, 42*(5), 266–275.

Richardson, D. (2012). Citizenship, nationality, and culture. In E. R. Meiners & Q. Therese (Eds.), *Sexualities in education: A reader* (pp. 219–228). New York: Peter Lang Publishing, Inc.

Romesburg, D., Rupp, L. J., & Donahue, D. M. (2014). *Making the framework FAIR: California history-social science framework proposed LGBT revisions related to the FAIR Education Act*. San Francisco, CA: Committee on Lesbian, Gay, Bisexual, and Transgender History.

Russell, S. T., Toomey, R. B., Crockett, J., & Laub, C. (2010). LGBT politics, youth activisim, and civic engagement. In L. R. Sherrod, J. Torney-Purta & C. A. Flanagan (Eds.), *Handbook of research on civic engagement in youth* (pp. 471–494). Hoboken, NJ: John Wiley & Sons, Inc.

Schmidt, S. J. (2014). Civil rights continued: How history positions young people to contemplate sexuality (in)justice. *Equity & Excellence in Education, 47*(3), 353–369.

Schmidt, S. J. (2015). A queer arrangement of school: Using spatiality to understand inequity. *Journal of Curriculum Studies, 47*(2), 253–273.

Stern, K. (Ed.). (2009). *Queers in history: The comprehensive encyclopedia of historical gays, lesbians, bisexuals, and transgenders*. Dallas, TX: BenBella Books, Inc.

Williams, T., Connolly, J., Pepler, D., & Craig, W. (2005). Peer victimization, social support, and psychosocial adjestment of sexual minority adolescents. *Journal of Youth and Adolescence, 34*(5), 471–482.

Young, I. M. (2000). *Inclusion and democracy*. New York: Oxford University Press.

6 Epilogue

Insisting that we use our common sense when reforming schools is really insisting that we continue to privilege only certain perspectives, practices, values and groups of people. Common sense is not what should shape educational reform or curriculum design; it is what needs to be examined and challenged.

(Kumashiro, 2009, p. xxxvi)

I have spent most of my academic career examining perspectives that are missing from curriculum in schools and searching for ways to increase perspectives in order to make curriculum more inclusive and critically democratic (e.g., Camicia, 2007, 2012; Camicia & Bayon, 2012; Camicia & Franklin, 2010; Camicia & Saavedra, 2009). My interest in this area is a product of my positionality and experiences. As illustrated in previous chapters, my positionalities and experiences serve as resources for inclusive curriculum because they provide narratives and counternarratives that challenge the oppression of 'common sense' in curriculum.

By providing counternarratives, the curriculum can facilitate examination of 'common sense' knowledge as it is implicated in inequitable power relations. The complicated conversations over curriculum that occur challenge taken-for-granted understandings by opening conversations to more choices and perspectives that have been drowned out by the din of dominant discourses. In this chapter, I conclude by examining some of the themes throughout the book by connecting them to my experiences with school and society.

Autoethnography is a method that I propose as a way to increase LGBTQ inclusion in curriculum. In recent publications, I have proposed the use of autoethnography as a way for teachers and students to understand the situated nature of knowledge and the ways that inequitable power relations structure curriculum (Camicia, 2014a, 2014b; Camicia & Di Stefano, 2015; Camicia & Zhu, 2012). This understanding supports the curriculum recommendations that I made in the last chapter surrounding Young's (2000) model for increasing inclusion as I apply it my curriculum proposal related to LGBTQ inclusion. In autoethnography, students and educators examine how their narratives are embedded in a network of power relations and discourses. By examining experiences as individual but also cultural and political, our bodies become sites for understanding how people's experiences and identities are expressions of culture and politics. Describing autoethnography and his process, Adams writes:

> I retrospectively write about personal experiences that stem from, or are made possible by, being a part of a culture and/or from embracing a particular cultural or personal identity. I distance myself from these experiences in an attempt to discern and analyze patterns of these experiences as evidenced by repeated characteristics, responses, feelings, and topics of discussion. In so doing, I make patterns of a culture familiar for insiders and outsiders, make personal experiences meaningful cultural experiences.
>
> (Adams, 2011, p. 159)

By using the method of autoethnography as a guide, the narratives and counternarratives of students, educators, and researchers can be the text of dialogue that sheds light on patterns of culture. This is particularly important when these patterns illustrate the ways that dominant cultures construct and maintain social inequalities inside and outside of schools. The narratives and patterns that emerge can challenge the taken-for-granted assumptions that reflect and maintain inequitable power relations within schools and society.

As I have mentioned throughout this book, an understanding of discourse and discursive fields helps to situate individual narratives and counternarratives within broader cultural and political structures. As seen in previous chapters, discourses provide opportunities and constraints for LGBTQ-inclusive curriculum. Discourses influence what can and can't be said in curriculum and beyond. Discourse defines what knowledge is valued and what knowledge is considered out of order and marginalized. As such, it can be used as a powerful tool for students and educators to examine 'common sense' claims of knowledge. The recommendations of educators throughout this book and the framework of inclusion provided by Young (2000) support discourse analysis within curriculum. I return to Hall's (2001) description of discourse as influencing:

how ideas are put into practice and used to regulate the conduct of others. Just as a discourse 'rules in' certain ways of talking about a topic, defining an acceptable and intelligible way to talk, write, or conduct oneself, so also, by definition, it 'rules out', limits and restricts other ways of talking, of conducting ourselves in relation to the topic or constructing knowledge about it.

(p. 72)

Discourses can support or challenge dominant ways of seeing schools and society because discourses do not act in isolation. They are located on a discursive field with other discourses (Camicia, 2014b; Spillman, 1995; Steinberg, 1998). For example, discourses of LGBTQ inclusion do not act in isolation. They interact on a discursive field with patriarchal and heteronormative discourses. The struggles between these different discourses are context dependent. As seen in the illustrations from California and Utah, what can and can't be said in curriculum about LGBTQ individuals looks very different in different contexts. The opportunities and constraints are unique to different discursive fields. Whereas discourses of LGBTQ inclusiveness can be stronger, as illustrated by examples from California, they also can be marginalized out of existence, as illustrated by examples from Utah.

Weedon (1999) writes that on a discursive field, discourses "are hierarchized by the relations of power which inhere within the discursive fields, privileging some versions and voices over others. Who and what is privileged is an ongoing site of political struggle" (p. 108). Discourses on discursive fields can perpetuate social justice or injustice depending upon the hierarchy of power relations within a given context. The individual narratives and counternarratives of students and educators can form the texts in which we can understand the hierarchies of discourses on discursive fields, and as a result, the relations of power that discourses reflect. As a way to see how students and teachers might incorporate autoethnography and discourse analysis into the curriculum, in the next section, I provide an example with my autoethnography.

An Autoethnography

Just as curriculum is not designed and implemented in an apolitical vacuum, so also research does not occur in an apolitical vacuum. As the researcher and writer of this book, I am embedded in historical and contemporary networks of power relations. My research interests, questions, and methods are a reflection of my location within these networks of power relations, and these networks influence my experiences and understanding of schools and society. As with all individuals, my knowledge is situated and unique, but also relational with larger social, cultural, and political patterns that can be discerned from this situatedness. This places situated knowledge as an important component of curriculum because it contributes to a larger understanding of society while valuing the knowledge that is specific to individuals. This rationale for situated knowledge is particularly important in social studies education where students learn the disciplines of geography, civics, history, and economics because these are areas that define what we have been, are, and will be in a relational sense. The more that we understand the situatedness of knowledge, the more we can communicate authentically within an ethics of recognition.

I write about my personal experiences and identities in the ways that I have proposed that students and educators communicate their experiences and identities within the curriculum. The narratives, counternarratives, and discourses that emerge can form the text of a curriculum that is relevant and challenges dominant ways of seeing schools and society. It is a curriculum that encourages the expression of the situated knowledge of students and educators as way to understand larger social, cultural, and political patterns within society.

My experiences and knowledge are the result of my body traveling historically and geographically and across different discursive fields. In these experiences, I learned from a very young age that times/places interact with power/knowledge and related discourses. Time/space, power/knowledge, and discourses have shaped me on the variety of discursive fields in which I have traveled throughout my life. Foucault (1977) writes:

> The body is the inscribed surface of events (traced by language and dissolved by ideas), the locus of a dissociated Self (adopting the illusion of a substantial unity), and a volume in perpetual disintegration. Genealogy, as an analysis of descent, is thus situated within the articulation of the body and history. Its task is to expose a body totally imprinted by history and the process of history's destruction of the body.
>
> (p. 148)

My positionality as White, male, cisgender, queer, English speaking, middle class, and U.S. citizen has located my body differently among the discursive fields that I have experienced throughout my life. My recognition of others and their recognition of me differs on different discursive fields because positionality is relational. As seen in previous chapters, the opportunities and constraints for recognition are contextual.

My earliest memories of the time/space formation and destruction of my body surrounded my awareness of discourses of masculinity and gender roles. From a very young age, I became physically ill when faced with competition. However, there were constant messages from a wide variety of sources ranging from school to media that, as a male, competition was a gauge that measured my normality or abnormality. The large size of my frame intensified my experiences with discourses of masculinity because my body seemed to be the perfect site for the inscription of discourses surrounding competition, strength, and violence. I was aware that discourses of masculinity operated on larger scales than my body. These larger scales were illustrated through, for example, media accounts in areas of history, politics, and sports.

However, my awareness, emotions, and understanding of the world were also influenced by discourses such as kindness and cooperation. However, these discourses rendered my body unrecognizable to most others because they did not reflect masculinities. In addition, I had little awareness that discourses of kindness and cooperation influenced other male bodies. These were not the messages sent by males in my close proximity or in larger society. The curriculum in my school and the books in my school library reinforced my isolation because there were no examples of people like me.

My earliest memory of the clash of these discourses on my body was in an early elementary school grade when my parents were called in to school because there was something abnormal about the way that I related to other boys. The message was clear. I needed to be fixed. Perhaps more football games or activities of violence would fix me? It was clear from an early age from everything to the study of history to the types of activities on the playground, I had little affinity with discourse of masculinity. How would the world look differently to me if the curriculum had recognized me for who I am? How would this change the way that I related to others?

A little later, but still below the age of 10, I had my first sexual encounter with another boy of similar age. Although I had little awareness of how strongly dominant society oppressed same-sex relationships, I was aware that I did not see any other same-sex relationships. The discourse of heteronormativity was ubiquitous on the discursive field of my childhood. In school, we did not read stories with characters in same-sex relationships. We did not see same-sex affection in public. We did not see movies with same-sex relationships. I didn't know enough to know what I didn't know, but I felt as if I had transgressed. I felt that my sexual feelings were something that I should be ashamed of. An adult found the other boy and I during a sexual encounter. My sense of our transgression was punctuated by the violent reaction of the adult who found us.

This added to the violence of the discursive field in which my body was embedded because the discourse of heteronormativity and other discourses of masculinity functioned to discipline my body to perform as a masculine heterosexual. I understood from a very young age that schools functioned unjustly by perpetuating and inscribing the discourses of society on the bodies of students. I was judged as sick, deficient, or less than human by the discourses that populated the discursive field in which I was embedded.

The discursive violence involved with these interactions intensified over the years. Whereas my experiences in early elementary grades involved "advice" from adults and verbal taunts and threats from other students, I experienced physical violence in the middle grades. The culmination of this latter form of violence occurred in a school locker room where one student assaulted me while other students cheered. It was a little after this point that I transferred schools. I started to perform masculinity and heterosexuality in order to alleviate my past suffering. Unfortunately, I came to realize that I was only replacing one type of suffering with another. For many years after this decision, I experienced the suffering of isolation and inauthenticity. It was a suffering that increased my life-threating depression. Because my large frame had intensified the power to inscribe masculine discourses upon my body, my body type had made the performance of discourses of masculinity believable or at least recognizable to others. Ironically, my recognition by others was accomplished by a fundamental misrecognition.

With the performance of my new identities, I experienced a new form of violence. The seventies were a time of great strides in lesbian and gay political power in San Francisco (Faderman, 2015; Hirshman, 2012; Shilts, 2008). The town that I grew up in is about 30 miles northeast of San Francisco. As some of the educators I interviewed mentioned, California has regional differences regarding the degree of support for the LGBTQ community. I experienced this in my youth. My first awareness of these regional differences was in middle school. Other male students at my school talked openly about how they had gone to San Francisco to assault gay men. They spoke about it with a great deal of pride. Inwardly, I felt as if they were talking about assaulting me. Their discourses of homophobia and violence intensified my silence and isolation, but as a result of their stories, I knew that there were other discursive fields where people thought and acted differently toward the LGBTQ community. There were places where discourses of recognition were supported.

The community that I grew up in near San Francisco was predominantly White and middle class. Dominant discourse reflected the demographics of the community that I knew. This meant discourses of race, ethnicity, and class were rarely discussed. The racism and classism that structured the community were veiled by a veneer of the 'taken for granted'. The history that I learned about in school reflected discourses of European and U.S. exceptionalism that placed White males as the norm toward which the rest of the world would be named and judged.

I continued my silence surrounding my sexuality through my high school years, and depression was a constant struggle. I performed in the ways that made me recognizable to the dominant culture and its discourses. I competed in swimming and water polo, and I had numerous female friends. Every once in a while I experienced the fear of being found out, such as the time that my gym teacher caught me looking at other male students or holding on to peers a little longer than necessary in contact sports. This same teacher roared at me in front of all the other students in my class, "Are you gay?" There it was; the discourse of homophobia was policing masculine and heteronormative boundaries.

Part of my high school time was spent in Hong Kong. This was a time when my awareness of discourses of racism, nationalism, and privilege increased. Whereas in my youth I was relatively unaware of my unearned privileges as a White, male, U.S. citizen, the three years that I spent in Hong Kong helped me gain an awareness of the discourses of racism and nationalism. I had moved to a different discursive field from the one of my youth. The discourse of nationalism was very different when living in a British colony. Colonization combined discourses of nationalism and racism in ways that were apparent to me in high school. My understandings of history, geography, and economics were shaped by a new discursive field. I also gained an awareness that the perspectives that people communicate are different on different discursive fields. The opportunities and constraints to talk about people and issues changed within different contexts and locations on the globe.

After graduating from high school, I attended and received a B.A. in Classics from San Francisco State University (SFSU). The SFSU discursive field in which I was embedded was different from any of the past discursive fields that I experienced. New discourses had more strength, whereas old discourses had diminished. This was apparent in the increased number of out people who I knew and the conversations about gender and sexuality that we openly spoke about. Whereas in the past I had only been embedded in discursive fields where discourses of homophobia and heteronormativity regulated thoughts and speech, this new discursive field contained new discourses that challenged oppressive discourses.

I began to be aware of the connection between language and power. I knew that texts and thoughts were not neutral and they often functioned to maintain social inequalities. There were many opportunities for me to come out during my time at SFSU because I had very close friends who were out, but my past experiences and my fear of losing family connections kept me from being out.

After graduation, I became a carpenter and eventually married a woman whom I lived with for 20 years. During this time, I struggled with at times debilitating depression and frequent thoughts of suicide. The discourses of my youth reemerged on the discursive fields of future places that I lived. Homophobic, racist, sexist, and nationalistic discourses intensified in the commercial construction workplaces that I spent most of my twenties and thirties. Whenever I openly resisted these discourses with counterdiscourses, reactions were swift and violent. These discursive fields perpetuated patriarchy, White privilege, and heteronormativity. This environment took its toll on my body and my health suffered. I knew that I had to switch discursive fields.

I enrolled in night school to become an elementary school teacher. During the days I was part of the construction site discursive field, and during nights I was part of the pre-service elementary teacher discursive field. Discourses of competition and violence during the day were replaced with discourses of cooperation and kindness during the night. The discourse of racism during the day was replaced with the discourse of antiracism at night. In addition, it was typical for males to comprise only 10 percent of the students in my courses, a percentage that would eventually reflect the demographics of schools where I taught. Many of the discursive fields of my past only allowed for one emotion as a male: anger. The discursive field of elementary education aligned with some of my earliest memories of where I wanted to be embedded. I did not experience fear when I spoke of my emotions or compassion toward others and myself. The dissonance between the discursive fields of day and night helped me see further connections between language and power.

As an elementary school teacher, I became interested in fostering discourses of inclusion within my classroom. I started reading the work of Walter Parker (1996, 2002, 2003) related to democratic education. In my sixth-grade classrooms, I started to facilitate regular class meetings and other instructional methods that would increase student engagement and voice within the curriculum. We discussed rules, behaviors, current events, and our individual roles within our classroom community. Although students often experienced an education system where the discourses of competition, standardization, and testing were ubiquitous, I planned and implemented curriculum that fostered discourses of cooperation and creativity. We explicitly examined discourses of racism, sexism, and classism. I was too fearful at that time to discuss discourses of homophobia, transphobia, or heteronormativity.

I was encouraged by the results of my curriculum. Students started to make connections between the responsibilities of individual students to the classroom community, but they also made connections between the classroom community's responsibilities to each student. The incidents of violent behaviors between students went down and student engagement with discourses of inclusion increased. This was evident in the content of class meetings and writing surrounding their personal experiences and their experiences with literature. Weaving inclusion and recognition throughout the curriculum increased student discourses of inclusion.

Through my experience with the discursive field we created in our classroom, I knew it was possible to create critical democratic communities within classrooms. Although I did not know about the concept of discourses and discourse analysis until a few years later, I now look back on our class discussions as including a form of discourse analysis. We looked at multiple perspectives through our experiences and the experiences of people we read about. We examined inequitable power relations that served to privilege dominant social groups. We discussed ways to talk and behave toward each other that would reduce these inequalities. I wanted to learn more about how this might work so I enrolled in a PhD program at the University of Washington (UW) so that I could study with my mentor, Walter Parker.

The discursive field of Seattle was much different than the discursive field of Reno, Nevada, where I taught elementary school. My courses at UW focused on multicultural, democratic, and global education. The discourses at UW were of inclusion and social justice. I was first introduced to the concept of discourses and a discursive field. Although the discursive field was dominated by a discourse of social justice, we also experienced a proliferation of discourses that strengthened the discourse of social justice. Discourses related to critical race theory, feminist epistemologies, queer theory, and postcolonial theory were powerful, and I understood that within each of these discourses there were many, many more discourses that supported counternarratives. Although related to the discourses that I tried to increase with students in my sixth-grade classrooms, the UW discursive field provided the opportunity and language to express these discourses.

After earning my PhD in curriculum and instruction, I started my position as an assistant professor at Utah State University (USU). I was still closeted at that point in my life. I had never lived in a community as religiously conservative as in Utah. I was fearful that my views would not be accepted, but I experienced an administration and faculty that was very supportive. Discourses of inclusion were powerful. Although supported in this way, I experienced the dominant discourses of Utah that I have already illustrated in previous chapters. The isolation that these discourses enforced and my recurring depression reached a climax. I knew that if I did not come out and live authentically, I would not survive the year.

At that time, no one who I spoke to knew of any out male faculty members. I came out and decided to divorce my wife. I was fearful of how my students would evaluate my teaching performance after I came out. Bad evaluations would undermine my ability to get tenure or be promoted. I also worried about my safety. During this time there were some very public comments by Mormon Church leaders condemning same-sex relationships. The discourse of homophobia increased its power during these public statements. As I have already discussed, this discourse has intensified, as evidenced in a fall 2015 denunciation of same-sex relationships and prohibitions on children in households with same-sex relationships. Although there are religious discourses of compassion, they are discourses that serve to dehumanize LGBTQ individuals as abnormal, deficient, and sick.

I married my husband, another USU professor, in 2011. We feel isolated by the discourse already mentioned and the effects they have on our community of Cache Valley, where USU is located. The effects of the discursive field are evident in the lack of visibility of LGBTQ individuals or issues. Although there are LGBTQ-inclusive student groups on campus, our role as faculty limits our interactions with these groups. Due to our isolation, we decided to move to Salt Lake City, where, as I already mentioned, the discursive field for adults is LGBTQ inclusive.

My narrative serves as text for me to examine how the discursive fields in which I have traveled have regulated my speech, thoughts, and actions. I use this as an example of how students and educators can open conversations that examine the discursive fields of their experiences and the experiences of others. These complicated conversations open third spaces where discourses of 'common sense,' 'normality,' and 'exclusion' are challenged. By examining different discursive fields, students and educators are better equipped to understand the knowledge/power relationship. Attention to this relationship can increase awareness of undemocratic communities in classrooms and beyond. Social studies subjects such as geography, civics, history, and economics take on a new and transformative dimension when discourses of inclusion are woven throughout the curriculum. This is education for critical democracy and LGBTQ inclusion.

References

Adams, T. E. (2011). *Narrating the closet: An autoethnography of same-sex attraction*. Walnut Creek, CA: Left Coast Press, Inc.

Camicia, S. P. (2007). Deliberating immigration policy: Locating instructional materials within global and multicultural perspectives. *Theory and Research in Social Education, 35*(1), 96–111.

Camicia, S. P. (2012). An ethics of recognition in global and teacher education: Looking through queer and postcolonial lenses. *International Journal of Development Education and Global Learning, 4*(1), 25–35.

Camicia, S. P. (2014a). My pedagogical creed: Positionality, recognition, and dialogue in democratic education. In S. Totten (Ed.), *The importance of teaching social issues: Our pedagogical creeds* (pp. 166–175). New York: Routledge.

Camicia, S. P. (2014b). Navigating/embodying controversy in classrooms in the United States and Philippines: Using autoethnography to understand the complexities of democracy in different contexts. In T. Misco & J. De Groof (Eds.), *Cross-cultural case studies of teaching controversial issues: Pathways and challenges to democratic citizenship education* (pp. 95–109). Oisterwijk, Netherlands: Legal Wolf Publishers.

Camicia, S. P., & Bayon, A. (2012). Curriculum development collaboration between colonizer and colonized: Contradictions and possibilities for democratic education. In T. C. Mason & R. J. Helfenbein (Eds.), *Ethics and international curriculum work: The challenges of culture and context* (pp. 73–92). Charlotte, NC: Information Age.

Camicia, S. P., & Di Stefano, M. (2015). Positionality and glocal encounters in social studies teacher education. In D. Schwarzer & B. Bridglall (Eds.), *Promoting global competence & social justice in teacher education* (pp. 279–297). Lanham, MD: Lexington Books.

Camicia, S. P., & Franklin, B. (2010). Curriculum reform in a globalised world: The discourses of cosmopolitanism and community. *London Review of Education, 8*(2), 93–104.

Camicia, S. P., & Saavedra, C. (2009). A new childhood social studies curriculum for a new generation of citizenship. *The International Journal of Children's Rights, 17*, 501–517.

Camicia, S. P., & Zhu, J. (2012). Synthesizing multicultural, global, and civic perspectives in the elementary school curriculum and educational research. *The Qualitative Report, 17*, 1–19.

Faderman, L. (2015). *The gay revolution: The story of the struggle*. New York: Simon and Schuster.

Foucault, M. (1977). Nietche, genealogy, history. In D. F. Bouchard (Ed.), *Language, counter-memory, practice: Selected essays and interviews by Michel Foucault* (pp. 139–164). Ithaca, NY: Cornell University Press.

Hall, S. (2001). Foucualt: Power, knowlege, and discourse. In M. Wetherell, S. Taylor & S. J. Yates (Eds.), *Discourse theory and practice: A reader* (pp. 72–81). London: SAGE Publications.

Hirshman, L. (2012). *Victory: The triumphant gay revolution.* New York: Harper-Collins Publishers.

Kumashiro, K. K. (2009). *Against common sense: Teaching and learning toward social justice* (2nd ed.). New York: RoutledgeFalmer.

Parker, W. C. (Ed.). (1996). *Educating the democratic mind.* Albany, NY: State University of New York Press.

Parker, W. C. (Ed.). (2002). *Education for democracy: Contexts, curricula, assessments.* Greenwich, CT: Information Age Publishing.

Parker, W. C. (2003). *Teaching democracy: Unity and diversity in public life.* New York: Teacher's College Press.

Shilts, R. (2008). *The mayor of Castro Street: The life and times of Harvey Milk.* New York: St. Martin's Griffen.

Spillman, L. (1995). Culture, social structures and discursive fields. *Current Perspectives in Social Theory, 15,* 129–154.

Steinberg, M. W. (1998). Tilting the frame: Considerations on collective action framing from a discursive turn. *Theory and Society, 27*(6), 845–872.

Weedon, C. (1999). *Feminism, theory and the politics of difference.* Malden, MA: Blackwell Publishers Inc.

Young, I. M. (2000). *Inclusion and democracy.* New York: Oxford University Press.

Index